MARCUS RASHFORD

HEROES

HOW TO TURN INSPIRATION INTO ACTION

Somerhill Book Day

2024

Awarded to

Jago Redman

Y4 Costume Parade Winner

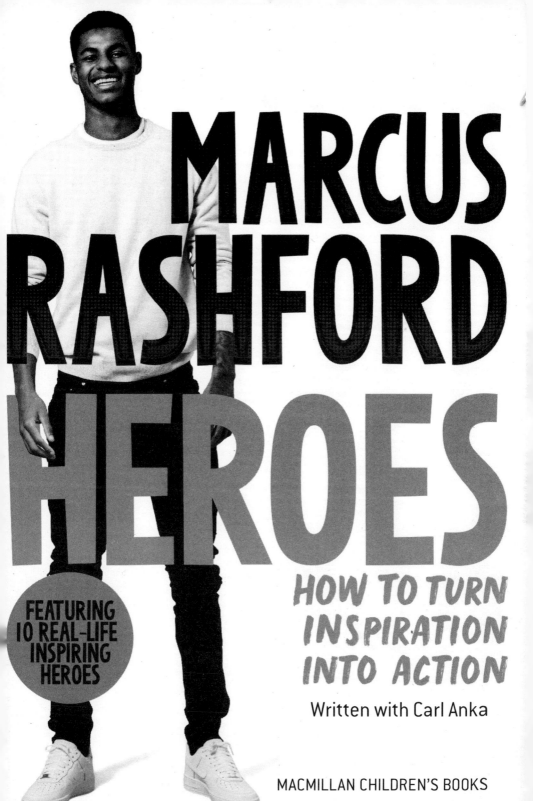

MARCUS RASHFORD

HEROES

HOW TO TURN INSPIRATION INTO ACTION

FEATURING 10 REAL-LIFE INSPIRING HEROES

Written with Carl Anka

MACMILLAN CHILDREN'S BOOKS

Published 2023 by Macmillan Children's Books
an imprint of Pan Macmillan
The Smithson, 6 Briset Street, London EC1M 5NR
EU representative: Macmillan Publishers Ireland Ltd, 1st Floor,
The Liffey Trust Centre, 117–126 Sheriff Street Upper
Dublin 1, D01 YC43
Associated companies throughout the world
www.panmacmillan.com

ISBN 978-1-0350-0664-9

3 5 7 9 8 6 4 2

A CIP catalogue record for this book is available from the British Library.

Printed and bound by CPI Group (UK) Ltd, Croydon CR0 4YY
Designed by Janene Spencer

OTHER BOOKS BY MARCUS RASHFORD

NON-FICTION

You Are a Champion
Written with Carl Anka

You Can Do It
Written with Carl Anka

The Marcus Rashford You Are a Champion Action Planner
Written with Katie Warriner

FICTION

The Breakfast Club Adventures series
Written with Alex Falase-Koya, illustrated by Marta Kissi

The Breakfast Club Adventures: The Beast Beyond the Fence
The Breakfast Club Adventures: The Ghoul in the School
The Breakfast Club Adventures: The Phantom Thief

And, coming March 2024:
The Breakfast Club Adventures: The Treasure Hunt Monster

CONTENTS

HI FRIENDS,

MY NAME IS MARCUS RASHFORD, AND I WANT TO THANK YOU FOR PICKING UP THIS BOOK.

Some of you might know me as a footballer for Manchester United and England. I've been playing professional football since 2016, and during that time I've been lucky enough to meet people from all around the world – it's great, because I get to speak to people from lots of different backgrounds and hear their stories.

I often think about how lucky I am, not just to be able to play the sport I love every day, but because I get to meet so many exciting, interesting and inspirational people from all walks of life. It's taught me that every person in this world is varied, and that all of our stories and experiences are so different.

I'm fascinated by stories. All kinds. It doesn't matter if they're in books, in films, in songs, or whether they're stories that people tell me. I love them all!

ONE OF THE THINGS I LOVE ABOUT BOOKS IN PARTICULAR IS THAT YOU GET TO IMAGINE YOURSELF IN SOMEONE ELSE'S SHOES. And I think that's true about speaking to other people, too, and hearing what they have to say about their own life.

In 2020 I went out to speak to a lot of families who were struggling to put food on the table. At that point, there were a lot of people in the UK who needed help. After talking to lots of different people and listening to what they had to say, I worked closely with charities like FareShare and the Trussell Trust, who try to make sure that all people in the UK have access to food.

We wanted to make sure that children around the country were able to get the food they needed. During our campaign, and along with the help of the British public, we did something incredible — we managed to convince the British government to set up a summer food fund during the COVID-19 pandemic, which helped to get food to 1.3 million schoolchildren across the UK.

But taking action and trying to make a change was never something I could have achieved on my own.

I was inspired to try and work with these charities and join their amazing campaign to end child food poverty because of lessons I had picked up from my heroes growing up.

TO ME, A HERO IS SOMEONE WHO INSPIRES A PERSON TO WANT TO DO BETTER.

They are someone you can find anywhere — it might be an actor you've seen on TV or a sportsperson, but it could also be a family member or a friend. Heroes come in all shapes and sizes, and they will impact your life in many different meaningful ways.

I have a lot of heroes, and in this book, I want to talk to you about a few of them.

Each person in this book has influenced my life in so many ways, and they've all taught me important life lessons.

Some of them you might have already heard about. Some of them you might not be familiar with. But either way, that's OK.

I WANT YOU TO JOIN ME ON A JOURNEY WHERE WE LOOK AT PEOPLE WHOSE WORDS AND ACTIONS HAVE HELPED ME WHENEVER I'VE FELT A BIT LOST IN MY LIFE, SO THAT THEY MIGHT BE ABLE TO HELP YOU ON YOUR JOURNEY TOO.

There are people like my mum, who taught me the importance of helping people whenever possible and learning to be grateful for the good days. But she also taught me that it's important not to be too worried about the not-so-good days, too.

It also includes people like Sir Alex Ferguson, former manager of Manchester United football club, whose lessons on leadership and how to put together a winning team have shaped my approach to looking after my friends and making sure we work in the best way possible together.

I also want to tell you about Muhammad Ali. He was one of the greatest boxers of all time, but also someone who talked about the importance of peace and looking after those around you.

And there are a few more people in here too! I hope that these people will inspire you to make a difference. I hope that they will show you how to be the best version of yourself that you can possibly be.

And, once you've read it, can you try to do me a favour? Can you pass on the lessons I got from these heroes to the people around you?

These heroes have inspired me. And I hope they inspire you as well.

I also hope that you'll learn how to look to the people around you and take inspiration from them; I want to show you how you can start finding real-life heroes in your own life too.

AND THEN I HOPE, ONE DAY, YOU CAN INSPIRE OTHERS AROUND YOU.

LET'S GET STARTED.

DINA ASHER-SMITH

1

DO YOU HAVE A PASSION? IS THERE SOMETHING IN YOUR LIFE, LIKE A HOBBY, THAT YOU MAKE SPECIAL TIME FOR?

Maybe you go to band practice, or play football with your mates. It could be that you like going to museums, or playing FIFA, or doing art. It could be anything! It's important to find things that make you happy.

I want to start this book by talking about someone who's worked hard to be the very best she can possibly be in the thing that she's passionate about – her name is Dina Asher-Smith, and she's one of the fastest women in the world.

I like to use my summers to watch athletics. Life in football is pretty busy, and most years I only get two weeks off training. This usually happens in July, which tends to line up with summer athletics championships: the Olympics or the World Championships.

If the athletics is on, I make an effort to watch some of the best athletes in the world try to achieve the impossible. I remember exactly where I was when Usain Bolt broke the world record in the 100 metres during the 2008 Olympics, and I remember watching the 2019 World Championships, when Dina Asher-Smith won three medals. She was the first British woman to win three medals at a World Championships and the first to win a world title in a sprint event. She's one of the fastest British women to ever compete at the Olympics.

She's an amazing athlete and I love watching her race, because it's clear to see how much passion she brings to the sport.

You see, she's fantastic for what she does on the track, but it's the work that she does off the track that takes her to the next level. Dina understands the difference sport has made to her life, and she wants everyone to have the opportunity to find passion in athletics.

Lots of girls stop playing sports when they get into secondary school, and Dina has spent a lot of time trying to stop this trend – she goes into schools and gives talks to try to encourage girls to get into sports. She also works to raise money for extra PE equipment in schools around the country.

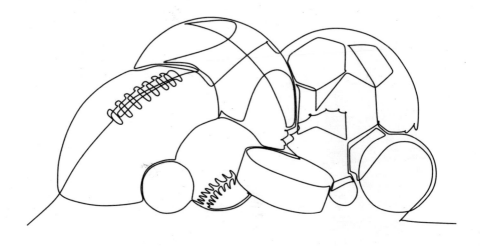

It's fantastic to hear her talk about the power of sport. But there is one particular moment from her career which really sticks out to me.

Going into the 2020 Olympics, Dina was regarded as one of the world's fastest women. She'd had a really good season that year and had bested some of the toughest competitors around. When everyone travelled to Tokyo for the Olympics that year, there were high expectations; everyone thought that she would win lots of medals and break world records.

Her plan was to compete in the 100 metres, 200 metres and then the 4 x 100 metres relay race with three other teammates. But, unfortunately, she didn't qualify for the 100-metre final – her performance in the semi-final heats just wasn't quick enough. Everyone watching at home was shocked. She'd had a brilliant season and was one of the favourites to win the medal, but she didn't even qualify for the final.

After the race, Dina did an interview. She explained that she had injured her hamstring earlier in the year in another competition, and that she wasn't able to perform at 100 per cent.

It was an emotional interview. Dina told us all that she wouldn't be able to compete in the 200 metres later on at the Olympics, either. She was clearly upset, as she had spent her whole life working towards this moment and dreamed of winning gold at the Olympics.

I remember watching that interview and feeling really bad for Dina, but listening to her speak was amazing. I remember she said:

WE TURNED OVER EVERY STONE TO STAND ON THE LINE. I'M SO GRATEFUL FOR EVERYBODY WHO PUT IN SO MUCH WORK FOR ME TO STAND ON THIS TRACK.

Even in one of the toughest moments in her career, Dina was able to appreciate all the work that she and her team had put in to get her to that point. She knew that she had done everything she could and had tried her very best, but she still wasn't going to achieve what she wanted. In one of the most disappointing moments of her career, Dina was still able to find something to celebrate, and thank others. That takes character. Thankfully, Dina was fit enough to compete in the 4 x 100 metres race, and her team won a bronze medal in the final!

In the years since, Dina has gone on to win lots of races, but she's also spoken about injuries and disappointments when competing. She wants to be the best in the world — as all athletes do — but she also knows the importance of finding a balance between working hard and looking after yourself.

And that's the reason that Dina Asher-Smith is one of my heroes. She works hard to be the very best that she can be, but she understands that life is all about balance. She knows when to work hard, and she knows when she has to stop. She listens to her body and takes care to look after both her mental health and her physical health.

Dina knows the importance of being the best you can be right *now*, rather than exhausting yourself trying to be the best in the world all of the time. She knows that she is only in competition with herself; that being the very best that she can be is about doing *her* best, not about beating others.

She's found a way to be successful in what she does *and* be happy away from the sport. She's never just been focused on training — she knows that the best way to improve in her sport is to have balance and care for her mental health.

WHAT'S KEY TO THAT IS LISTENING TO HER OWN BODY AND UNDERSTANDING WHAT IT NEEDS

When Dina is tired, she takes a break. When she's hungry, she makes sure she takes time to eat. When she's feeling bored or uninspired, she goes for a walk and makes an effort to do something she enjoys.

She has to work hard to be a great athlete — when she's training, she's locked in 100 per cent, giving the best she can — but Dina is great because she speaks openly about how her 100 per cent isn't going to be at the same level every day. We're all human, and we all have ups and downs. Dina is part of a new generation of athletes who talk about what it takes to look after themselves mentally and physically, and why that's so important. I think that's brilliant because all these athletes are sharing their message with the next generation, who will hopefully be inspired by what they say.

Every day I wake up and try to be the best I can be. There are days when I can do a lot, and there are days when, for lots of different reasons, I can't. Those days can be tough, but I try to keep in mind that all I can do is my best, and there's no point comparing myself to anyone else.

Dina is the same. Of course we both have to compete against other athletes, but the most important thing we do daily is test *ourselves* and see how high our talents can take us at that time.

I want to remind you that you are not trying to be better than the person next to you. You are not competing with your siblings, your friends or other people in your class.

BE THE
BEST VERSION
OF YOURSELF
THAT YOU CAN BE

But remember, when you're out there pushing yourself and trying to improve, try to find balance in the things you do. Be mindful of what your body and mind are trying to tell you. Dina doesn't race every day, and I don't play football seven days a week, 365 days a year. We both take days off to rest our bodies so that we can peak at the right moments. It's important for us — all of us, including the ones reading this book — to take days off to relax and care for ourselves.

And, when you're having a moment to yourself, take some time to think about your mental health. I want you to know that talking to someone and opening up to them doesn't make you weak — it will make you stronger. If you are struggling, find someone to talk to.

Something I try to do in my life is make special note of the things that make me happy. If I find myself doing something that brings a smile to my face, I try to remember who I'm with and think about whether or not I can do it again soon. That way, if there are times when I'm not so happy, I know what sort of things I can do to get my smile back.

Could you try that? It might sound strange, but the next time you're out, practising one of your hobbies with your friends and you find yourself having fun, why don't you say out loud . . .

THIS IS FUN.
I'M HAVING FUN

You might be surprised by what your friends say back.

I hope your journey is packed with as much success and joy as Dina's has, but I also hope you can take heart from the way she always looks to find balance in her life. She may not have won the medals she wanted to at the 2020 Olympics, but she was able to take pride in simply getting to an event that she dreamt of many, many years before. There are times when life gives you a tough road to walk down, but Dina has been brilliant at explaining how to walk down those paths without getting too downbeat.

There's more than one way of winning, and it's important to celebrate all of the little wins whenever they come. And if you want to find more wins on your journey, remember that the journey is all about balance.

MAKE SURE YOU TAKE BREAKS AND LET YOURSELF RELAX

REMEMBER

THAT YOU ARE ONLY IN COMPETITION WITH

YOURSELF

IF YOU CAN DO THAT, YOU CAN DO ANYTHING.

LEBRON JAMES

2

*I WANT TO TALK TO YOU ABOUT MY FAVOURITE
BASKETBALL PLAYER IN THE WORLD.*

His name is LeBron James.

Growing up in Manchester, I didn't know too much about basketball,
but I picked up a few things in PE lessons and watched bits on TV or
YouTube. Just like in football, there are
basketball players from all over
the world, all with different
skills and favourite positions.
And the very best basketball
players play in the biggest
basketball league in the
world, called the NBA —
the National
Basketball
Association.

LeBron James has been playing in the NBA for TWENTY years. During that time he's won four Championships and has played some of the best basketball the world has ever seen.

To be a great basketball player you need to be really determined. You have to be able to push yourself constantly and find ways to help your team score. You must also be a good defender and work hard to stop the opposition from scoring too many points.

A good NBA player is confident and can perform on the biggest occasions, against the toughest opponents. They're brave and they don't let nerves affect their performance. They also have to be a good communicator so that their teammates know what they're doing on the court, and what their plans are. (Some basketball players even speak in code on the court, so the other team can't figure out what attacking moves they will try!)

BUT MOST OF ALL, A GOOD BASKETBALL PLAYER IS
ADAPTABLE

That's because basketball is one of the fastest team sports in the world. In the NBA there is something called a shot clock – *IT MEANS THAT A TEAM HAS TO TRY AND SCORE IN FEWER THAN TWENTY-FOUR SECONDS EVERY TIME THEY START A MOVE*. This means you have to play quickly. It also means you have to think quickly too. The best basketball players are running about the court, passing, moving, shooting and dribbling in short, sharp bursts. They're constantly taking in information and looking to make the best plans to help their team win. Those plans change constantly based on the score, who is on the court and how much time is left in the game.

A good basketball player might have one outstanding talent. But the very best players have many different talents, and they can use different skills when the time calls for it.

That's what I like about LeBron James. It's not just that he's got a lot of different basketball skills. It's that he's constantly learning and adapting and pushing himself to be the best that he can possibly be.

Let me show you what I mean. Very early in his career, people said that LeBron was good at scoring close to the hoop, but he needed to work on his shooting when he was further away from it. Rather than focus on what he was already good at, scoring close to the hoop, he went away and worked really hard on the part that he could improve on – shooting from far away. After that, people said he wasn't the best when facing basketball players who were taller than him. So he contacted some experts who'd won basketball titles in the 90s so that he could learn from them.

Whenever people said that LeBron had a weak point in his game, he worked and trained until that weakness became one of his strengths. He was constantly being adaptable. Think about it – it's one thing to be the best basketball player in a single year, but LeBron has been one of the world's best for twenty years!

I don't think you can become great at something just by thinking you're the best.

THE MOMENT YOU START THINKING YOU'RE THE BEST IS OFTEN WHEN YOU START GETTING TOO COMFORTABLE, AND STOP TRYING TO TEST YOURSELF.

And when you do that, other teams and individuals will catch up.

When you play team sports like basketball or football, the opposition always looks for ways to stop your best skills and throw you off your game. So you have to learn how to adapt and find ways to be effective, regardless of what is going on. If you can't adapt and change with the times or styles of play, you will eventually struggle.

As a kid, I tried the same technique every time I played tic-tac-toe against my siblings. It worked for a while, and there was a point where I would win every game by using these same tactics, but soon enough my siblings realised what I was doing. Once they learned that, it was easy enough for them to stop me before I could get three in a row. If I wanted to win, I had to change my approach. I'm telling you this because I want you to know that

ADAPTABILITY
IS KEY FOR SO MANY DIFFERENT PARTS OF LIFE.

LeBron James has been able to adapt to different game plans for nearly TWENTY years, and in that time he's managed to win four NBA Championships across three different teams. To win even one NBA title is an incredible achievement, but winning multiple Championships, across so many years, makes him stand out as one of the best players around.

A lot of people think LeBron James is the Greatest Basketball Player of All Time. I think so too, but I have extra reasons for LeBron being my favourite.

Because LeBron isn't just amazing for the stuff he does on the basketball court. He's amazing for what he does off the court, too.

You see, LeBron is more than just a basketball player — he's also an activist and a supporter of many different charitable causes.

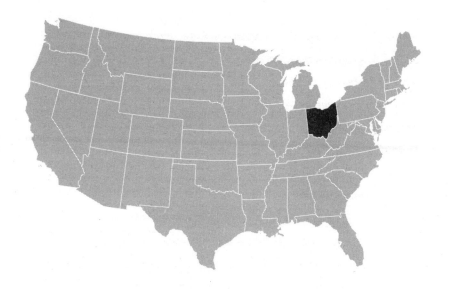

LeBron grew up in a city called Akron in the state of Ohio in the United States. Akron is an area where there are problems with crime and other issues, and over the years LeBron has worked incredibly hard to improve things for the next generation in his hometown. In 2004 – only one year after he started his career in the NBA – he set up the LeBron James Family Foundation. This foundation has the goal of helping families in Akron by improving schools, transport and other services in the area, and LeBron has donated a huge amount of his time and money to help support afterschool clubs, help students get scholarships to colleges, and more. The Akron of today is a better place to live than the Akron that LeBron grew up in, and a lot of that is due to the work done by the foundation.

LeBron James is adaptable, not just in how he plays basketball, but also in how he uses the sport as a force for good in his community. He's helped create his own basketball league for children and he supplies them with their own jerseys, so that they don't have to worry about spending money on bringing their own kits from home. When kids play in LeBron's league it looks and feels professional. It helps show them that with a bit of talent and a lot of hard work, they might one day become good basketball players too.

LeBron's charitable work goes beyond just the jerseys though. He's donated loads of shoes to people in the community, whether it's people who'd like to start playing basketball or people who need help to walk to school, or in the park. It's one of those small, important things that LeBron always thinks of. When you have a good, comfortable and dependable pair of shoes then getting around your area is much, much easier. You don't have to worry about walking to school or walking to work. You don't spend so much time worrying about the effects of rain or bad weather ruining your shoes. If you're someone who walks about a lot (or plays a lot of sport) having a good pair of shoes is essential to everything you do. LeBron understands that.

LeBron's work goes beyond the city of Akron and into the wider area too. He spent years playing for a basketball team called the Cleveland Cavaliers. They were an NBA team near Akron, and he became a hometown hero to fans there, helping them win their first ever Championship in 2016. But on top of that he also helped build a school in Cleveland to help disadvantaged children. The school is called 'The I Promise School'. It got its name because it's a promise from LeBron to look after the children who attend the school, and in turn it's a promise from all its pupils to try and be the best they can be.

That's what LeBron does; he speaks up for causes he feels strongly about and tries his best to help where possible. Over the years I've watched him take part in anti-bullying and anti-racism campaigns, as well as speak about the importance of clean food and water for those who need it most.

This work has earned him critics over the years — many people think he should just stick to playing basketball, and tell him to be quiet 'and just dribble', but LeBron never lets what other people say get to him. When he believes in something he keeps his head up and tries his hardest to do things as best as he can. That says a lot about his character; he is someone who has worked hard to get where he is in life, but he wants to make sure the journey for the next generation isn't as difficult.

He's going to go down in history not just for his incredible basketball skills, but also for how he helps others.

I'm lucky enough to have met LeBron and let me tell you, he is really tall.

Like, really, **REALLY** tall.

I like to think of myself as tall, but I looked tiny when I stood next to him! The first time we shook hands I couldn't believe it!

He's an amazing athlete, and he's also got an amazing mind too. He understands how important it is to be adaptable in sports and life, but he knows that the most important thing is having a big heart. I think LeBron's passion for what he does drives him to want to be the best. His love of basketball pushed him to learn many different skills and become better and better at playing the game. His love of Akron pushed him to become more and more outspoken about what he believed in, and helped him focus on making things better for the next generation.

He's also really funny and kind. He's always advising people to push themselves, do what they love and never give up. When we met we spoke about the importance of giving back to your local community, and why you need to be adaptable when you do it.

There is rarely just one reason why it's difficult for some children to go to school, or just one way that people can clean up their neighbourhoods. And this means you can rarely solve the issue with just one idea.

When LeBron first wanted to give children in Akron the opportunity to get into basketball, he thought the solution was to build more courts. But then he noticed the problems occurring close to those courts and looked to improve the area as a whole. Then he looked at how children travelled from their homes to the courts, and he wanted to make those routes safer. Then he wanted to make sure that anyone who wanted to play had a better pair of shoes. And after he did that, he tried to help out in the schools, so that the kids who wanted to get better at learning how to play basketball had the help they needed, with the sport and other things too. LeBron was constantly adapting to the needs of his community, because he realised that there wasn't just one way to help — there were tons of different approaches that he needed to try.

The very best basketball players have many talents and can rely on different skills when the time calls for it. The very best role models and helpers in the community will have loads of different ways to help out when the time calls for it.

I try to take inspiration from that. I know that my love of football has put me on an incredible journey, and that journey has given me a love for the people who helped me get to where I am today. I try to repay that love daily, by giving back to my community and the people who have helped me along the way.

I want you to try to take inspiration from LeBron James too. For me, he's amazing because he has shown the world there's more than one way to be great. *IT'S NOT JUST FROM PLAYING SPORTS, BUT FROM THE MANY DIFFERENT FORMS OF KINDNESS HE SHOWS TO OTHERS AROUND HIM.*

It's really important that you try to be adaptable in your own life — and there are loads of different ways to do this!

BEING ADAPTABLE MEANS THAT YOU ARE ALWAYS FINDING DIFFERENT WAYS TO IMPROVE YOURSELF AND THE WORLD AROUND YOU.

Very often in my life, I find that there is more than one way to get something done, so sometimes it's good to try alternative routes. If you're someone who can find reading hard, why don't you adapt and try listening to audiobooks?

I have someone in my life who doesn't like having to run when they do exercise, so they adapted and started cycling instead.

When I'm playing football, and the defender is being really aggressive and tackling me early to stop me from running past them, I often try to adapt and pass around them quickly so they can't catch me!

That's what being adaptable is about. It's thinking:

THIS TECHNIQUE ISN'T WORKING FOR ME RIGHT NOW, SO CAN I DEVELOP SOMETHING ELSE TO GET THE RESULTS I WANT?

If you're finding something particularly hard, whether learning a new skill in a sport, a lesson at school, or working with a new teammate, try approaching it in a new way.

CAN YOU TRY A DIFFERENT WAY TO LEARN THAT NEW SKILL?

CAN YOU SPEAK TO YOUR TEACHER ABOUT THE LESSON YOU'RE STRUGGLING IN, AND ASK THEM TO HELP YOU?

CAN YOU TALK TO YOUR TEAMMATE AND FIND OUT HOW THEY LIKE TO WORK TOGETHER, AND SEE IF YOU CAN FIND A WAY FORWARD FROM THERE?

One of the best ways to adapt and change your approach is to research it or to ask for advice. And asking someone for help will always help you on your journey.

THERE IS NEVER JUST ONE
WAY TO DO SOMETHING — AND
LEBRON JAMES IS PROOF OF THAT.
LOOK HOW SUCCESSFUL HE'S BEEN ON
THE BASKETBALL COURT AND WITH
HIS COMMUNITY WORK! HIS ADAPTABILITY
HAS HELPED HIM TO DREAM BIG AND
ACHIEVE SO MUCH, AND I KNOW THAT IF
YOU TRY HARD TO BE ADAPTABLE TOO
YOU WILL BE ABLE TO DO SO MANY
AMAZING THINGS.

BEYONCÉ

WHEN I WAS GROWING UP, THERE WAS ALWAYS MUSIC PLAYING IN MY HOUSE.

Everyone in my family loves music, and there would always be lots of different types playing on the radio or on the CD player (which probably makes me sound really old to you, but remember we didn't have anything like Spotify back then!).

I liked listening to hip-hop and grime with my brothers. My mum would listen to things like Motown, R&B and soul.

And my sisters. My sisters loved listening to Beyoncé.

And I mean they LOVED listening to Beyoncé. In 2008, she released an album called *I Am . . . Sasha Fierce*, and my sisters would play it over

and over and over again. It's got some of the most iconic Beyoncé songs of all time on it – things like 'Halo', 'Single Ladies' and 'If I Were a Boy'. I don't think I went a week that year without hearing it in the house!

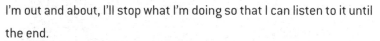

I didn't mind too much though. It's a great album, and it made my sisters happy. Even now, if I hear a song from that album when I'm out and about, I'll stop what I'm doing so that I can listen to it until the end.

That's one part of what makes Beyoncé so great; she creates songs that can stop you in your tracks.

It feels a bit strange having to explain why Beyoncé is fantastic for this chapter because, well . . .

SHE'S BEYONCÉ.

She's one of the biggest-selling and most well-known musicians of all time. She started her career in the 1990s in an R&B girl group called Destiny's Child. Together, they sold more than 60 million records around the world. Then, in the early 2000s, Beyoncé began to release music as a solo artist. And that took her career to a whole new level.

BECAUSE BEYONCÉ ISN'T JUST ONE OF THE BEST SINGERS IN THE WORLD. SHE'S ALSO ONE OF THE BEST DANCERS, ONE OF THE BEST SONGWRITERS, AND ONE OF THE BEST LIVE PERFORMERS. AND, ON TOP OF ALL THAT, SHE HAS CREATED SOME OF THE BEST MUSIC VIDEOS OF ALL TIME.

She has so many achievements that belong in the record books: **SHE'S SOLD MORE THAN 200 MILLION RECORDS WORLDWIDE, SHE'S WON THIRTY-TWO GRAMMY AWARDS, AND SHE'S HAD THE NUMBER-ONE SONG IN THE UNITED STATES THIRTY-ONE TIMES. SHE WAS THE FIRST SOLO ARTIST TO HAVE THEIR FIRST SEVEN STUDIO ALBUMS DEBUT AT NUMBER ONE IN THE UNITED STATES.**

What's more, she has also used her profession to help others, spread social justice awareness and inspire the next generation. From time to time, I rewatch a music video she made with the United Nations called 'I Was Here', where she travels to developing nations all around the world and talks about the importance of building schools and wells, so that children can have access to clean water. She's an excellent example for the next generation; she's talented, she believes in herself and she wants those who come after her to do the same as well.

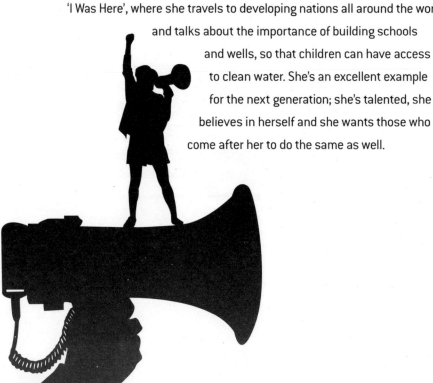

Beyoncé is so good at her craft that you only need to refer to her by her first name, and everyone understands who you're talking about. There's only one Beyoncé in the world because there aren't many musicians who have ever been able to match her talent.

SHE IS ABSOLUTELY ONE OF A KIND

I think lots of people look at Beyoncé and think that she's lucky to be so talented. But the truth is that talent rarely comes without a lot of hard work, and Beyoncé's success didn't happen overnight. She's put an incredible amount of time and energy into getting where she is now. And what's really special about Beyoncé, what makes her unique – and what makes so many people stop and listen to her songs – is how inventive she is.

If you've ever listened to a Beyoncé song, the first thing that stands out is how good her voice is. Beyoncé can hit musical notes that most people can only *dream of*. And, like I said above, she wasn't born able to do that. She can do that because she has worked *really* hard. Beyoncé has been taking singing lessons since she was a child, and even now she still practises her singing for hours a day. As a result, she has a way of hitting high notes that really sit with you.

ON TOP OF THAT, SHE'S WORKED HARD TO BE ABLE TO SING AND DANCE AT THE SAME TIME.

You see, when Beyoncé was getting started with Destiny's Child, people were already impressed by how good a dancer she was. Just like singing, she's been dancing since she was very young. And, when she was dancing with Destiny's Child, she wouldn't just pay attention to the dance instructors and learn how to do complicated routines; she wanted to be an impressive performer, and over time she learned how to create choreography of her own as well. Beyoncé did more than copy things the best in the music industry could come up with. She was able to learn from the best and apply her own spin on things.

She's always looking for creative ways to improve the things she's good at. She's a fantastic singer, but she's always looking for new ways to develop her voice and push her singing to different levels, whether by writing a difficult song or singing something she's not used to. Beyoncé isn't usually a rapper, but every now and then she'll do a song with her husband Jay-Z, and she ends up sounding like one of the world's best rappers! You can tell she studied the craft and looked at how to make the lyrics and the verses work together.

Another incredible thing about Beyoncé is how much attention she pays to how audiences respond to her worldwide. Beyoncé has played many shows in different countries, but she still finds a way to connect with people, even if she doesn't speak the same language as them. She's spent a lot of time learning about live performance – not just about how singers deal with nerves when performing in front of an audience, but she's also learned from professional sportspeople how to block out distractions in big moments and stay focused when it's time to perform.

When she put all her learnings together, it created an outstanding live performer who sells out concerts worldwide. Beyoncé tickets sell out in *minutes*, because fans know she will put on a jaw-dropping show.

She doesn't settle for being good in just one way. She always puts herself out there in the deep end. I think when people back themselves to do that, they excel.

The reason she's so talented is because she thinks outside the box — she makes an effort to learn and take inspiration from lots of different things around her. She's always looking for new inspirations and ways to be the best she possibly can be. Think about it — she was never just focused on singing. She knew there were many different ways she could work towards her goal, through studying sports, music and dance to incorporate into her work.

I am not as good a singer or a dancer as Beyoncé is (no one is!), but I take a lot of inspiration from how she constantly looks to improve and hone her craft.

For me, you don't improve by doing the same thing over and over again. You're not always going to get better by doing the same routine. I try to think outside the box when I want to get better at football. On top of doing skills and training with the team, I like to go out and speak to other people, and listen to what they have to say. Sometimes, just listening to or watching other individuals who play a similar position to me, or who've been in a similar situation to me in life, will help me get better. That's helped me improve in certain aspects; mixing up your training is important to make sure that you're always learning and taking on new information.

Whether you're trying to improve a physical skill or a mental skill, it's important to be imaginative while you do it.

IT DOESN'T MATTER HOW LONG THE PROCESS TAKES, **WHAT MATTERS IS THAT YOU'RE COMMITTED TO LEARNING AND DOING BETTER** JUST LIKE BEYONCÉ HAS BEEN THROUGHOUT HER CAREER.

So if you're reading this and wondering if I'm challenging you to be as talented as Beyoncé, don't worry. I understand that she is an exceptional, one-of-a-kind talent, and I don't want to put that sort of pressure on anyone.

What I do think you can do, though, is try to take a leaf out of Beyoncé's book. Think about how you can do things differently, and look to improve yourself based on what you find out. Like I said before, a lot of what makes her unique comes from how she takes inspiration from many different things around her to create her own style. She thinks outside the box.

What do you do when you're looking for inspiration? For me, it starts with the environment around me. When I'm looking for extra motivation, I try to go back and enjoy some of my favourite things and see if I can learn any new lessons from them.

Do you have a favourite book that you haven't read in a while? I sometimes go back to my favourite book with a pencil and reread it, highlighting the bits that get me thinking. The way I read some pages when I was fourteen is very different from how I read pages when I was eighteen, which is also different from how I read sentences now. Returning to old things you enjoy after a while is an excellent way to get the creative ideas flowing, as you can find newer perspectives as you get older.

Do you like writing? If so, make sure to read as much as you can, and then try writing in lots of different styles — it could be fiction, poetry, non-fiction or even music! If you like baking cakes, try some new recipes and make cookies or brownies for a change, and see what you learn. If you like a particular kind of dancing, make sure you find out about other types too, and see how they might help you get better at what you love.

Remember to look out for new inspirations also! Don't just read one kind of book, or only watch one genre of film, or listen to one type of music. It's always good to try new things, and you might be surprised at what you like. Take tips from everything you see and everyone you talk to. Like I've already said, don't just do the same things over and over again.

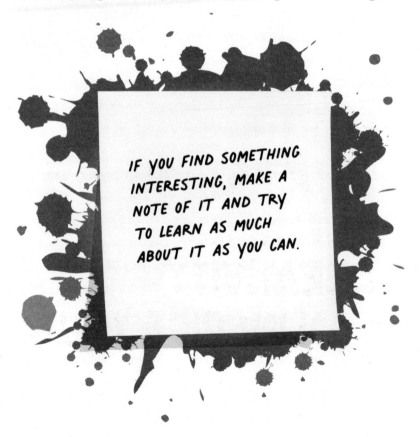

IF YOU FIND SOMETHING INTERESTING, MAKE A NOTE OF IT AND TRY TO LEARN AS MUCH ABOUT IT AS YOU CAN.

REMEMBER: THE GOAL ISN'T TO BECOME THE NEXT BEYONCÉ, BUT TO UNDERSTAND HOW HER CREATIVITY CAN INSPIRE YOU

THERE ARE MANY
DIFFERENT WAYS WE CAN ALL
LEARN AND BE CREATIVE, SO TAKE
HEART THAT YOUR WAY TO THE TOP
COULD BE COMPLETELY DIFFERENT. TAKE
PRIDE IN IT ALL. IT'S YOUR JOURNEY AND
YOU CAN DO WHATEVER YOU WANT WITH
IT, BUT WHEN YOU START TO THINK
OUTSIDE THE BOX AND APPROACH
THINGS CREATIVELY, AMAZING
THINGS CAN HAPPEN.

DENZEL WASHINGTON

4

I REALLY LIKE WATCHING FILMS.

I watch all sorts: animated films (I love the Ninja Turtles!), films about sport, westerns, science-fiction, action films . . . the works! If I ever get a bit of spare time I like to take myself to the cinema and watch whatever is on – I'm not picky! Sometimes I go with friends, but I really like going to the cinema on my own. I switch my phone off, stop thinking about football for a bit and just unwind, watching a great story.

I've got lots of favourite films, and over time I've started to pick out my favourite actors too. One of my favourite actors in the world is a guy called Denzel Washington. To me, he's the best actor around.

I've watched just about every single film Denzel has acted in. He's a really intelligent and magnetic actor. He's just so captivating in every role he plays — you can't help but pay attention to him, no matter what he's doing or how big the role is.

Denzel's played police officers, American football coaches, lawyers, pilots and many other roles. He's really good at transforming himself and making you feel like you're watching a real person. He plays a lot of people from history too, and has an incredible way of moving and speaking just like them. He'll memorise their speeches and get their mannerisms right, so you believe you're watching a history book come to life!

Denzel was the first African American to ever receive two Oscars (he's been nominated ten times overall!). He's won awards for being both the lead actor and in the supporting cast. That means that he's not just someone who does the big roles that draw a lot of attention. He's also brilliant at being a team player and keeping standards high. Tom Hanks — another great actor — once said that working with Denzel was like 'Going back to film school'. He's an actor who helps make other actors better and who wants to share his expertise. On top of that, Denzel is also a brilliant director who has helped to make films that have led other actors to win Oscars too.

After watching a few of Denzel's films, I wanted to find out more about him. I began to read about his life and about how he became such a talented actor.

One thing I found out – which I found really interesting – is that Denzel didn't initially want to become an actor. After he finished high school he went to university and studied biology, because at that point he wanted to become a doctor. After a while he changed his mind and swapped courses to study journalism. Then, in between classes, he started to do some drama lessons on the side.

It was those drama lessons that lit a fire in him. When he was at university Denzel took part in a number of plays. That's where he discovered that he loved to act. So, after graduating, he decided to move to Hollywood and give acting a go.

When Denzel was in Hollywood he met another actor called Sidney Poitier — another one of my heroes — who was the first Black man to ever win an Oscar for acting. Sidney would become a mentor to Denzel. He introduced him to other people who could help him in Hollywood, and helped him improve his craft. Years later, Denzel would become a mentor and teacher to the next generation of actors, showing them how they could become better actors as well.

DENZEL ONCE SAID,

I REMAIN THANKFUL FOR THE GIFTS THAT I'VE BEEN GIVEN AND I TRY TO USE THEM IN A GOOD WAY, IN A POSITIVE WAY

He recognises that he is one of the best actors in the world and knows that there are many people who look up to him — but he is always grateful, and he wants to be a role model to others and help lift up other people around him.

That's one of the great things about Denzel; he doesn't hide his talent or try to keep his knowledge about the acting industry a secret. Instead, he shares his skills and knowledge with other people so they can get better. There are a lot of interviews with great filmmakers and actors who like to talk about the lessons they've picked up when working with Denzel.

HE KNOWS THAT WHILST IT'S FUN TO BE GOOD AT SOMETHING, IT'S EVEN BETTER WHEN THOSE AROUND YOU ARE ALSO IMPROVING AND BECOMING GREAT IN THEIR OWN WAYS.

Denzel Washington is not someone to get jealous or annoyed when someone else beats him to an acting award, or if people say there are actors who are better than him at certain things. He knows what he is good at, and he knows the path that he wants to walk in life. He's confident in his abilities. He's able to be calm and enjoy moments of success in his life, but he also understands that *FAILURE IS A BIG PART OF THAT SUCCESS*.

It's Denzel's attitude towards failure that I find particularly interesting. He always talks about how failure is an essential part of any journey, because failing at something shows that you are trying and that you aren't afraid to take risks. He has always remembered the words of one of his old teachers, who said,

DON'T BE AFRAID TO FAIL BIG

'Failing big' is quite a confusing phrase. No one ever wants to embarrass themselves in public, or have a lot of people tell them that their best efforts weren't good enough. But being able to fail big is an important life skill.

Failing big is a bit different from giving up or not passing a test. It can sometimes feel like losing, but not every defeat means you are failing big. When you fail big, it means that you have tried your hardest and taken a risk, but for some reason things haven't worked out.

Let me try to explain. I lose in small ways **ALL OF THE TIME**:

WHEN I PLAY BOARD GAMES WITH MY SIBLINGS

WHEN I SLEEP THROUGH MY ALARM

OR IF I'M LATE TO MEET MY BROTHER FOR COFFEE

Those are small losses.

I have also lost in big ways in my life too. I've played in many cup finals and ended up with silver medals rather than the gold I hoped for. I failed to score a penalty in one of the most important games in the history of England's national team. These are the times that I have 'failed big'.

Mistakes happen. Small ones, that can get fixed in a day, but also big ones, which can sometimes take weeks – or even months – to get through.

But, like Denzel, I'm OK with that. I know that I am human and that humans make mistakes. I try not to let the losses – big or small – pile up and overwhelm me. To remember that there are good parts to everything, alongside the bad. The worst days of my life don't define me, and I don't want any of your bad days to define you.

I want to give you an example. I wasn't always the best football player. When I was younger I had to make many, many, *many* mistakes to improve my game. And I still do now! For every free kick I score, there are hundreds in training that I shoot off target. But I *want* to make mistakes because mistakes show that I am trying. They show that I am willing to take a risk. If I only ever tried to make the shots I know I can make, I wouldn't be a good footballer. I wouldn't be adapting my game, and I wouldn't ever get better.

EVERY SINGLE MISTAKE I HAVE MADE WHILE PLAYING FOOTBALL HAS MADE ME A BETTER PLAYER, BECAUSE I'VE HAD TO LEARN HOW TO DO BETTER NEXT TIME.

Denzel is exactly the same. Not every single film he has been in has been good. On top of that he's regretted turning down some roles that have ended up being really good for the person who stepped in instead.

But Denzel knows that *IF YOU WANT TO DREAM BIG, YOU MUST BE PREPARED TO 'FAIL BIG' TOO. YOU CAN'T ALWAYS GET THINGS RIGHT.* If you want to truly push yourself and try your best in life, you also have to open yourself up to being vulnerable and making mistakes.

That sounds scary, but some of the best things you can learn about yourself come after a loss. Think about it: Denzel is one of the greatest actors of all time . . . but he was only able to become an actor after he learned that being a doctor and being a journalist wasn't for him. Studying biology and journalism at university ended up being two big mistakes for him, but the lessons he learned along the way have helped him to become the actor, and the person, that he is today.

IF YOU SPEND YOUR
WHOLE LIFE TRYING TO AVOID
MISTAKES YOU WILL AVOID SOME
OF THE SMALL LOSSES IN YOUR LIFE.
BUT IF YOU ARE TOO SCARED OF
MAKING MISTAKES, YOU'RE GOING
TO MISS OUT ON LEARNING SOME
IMPORTANT LESSONS.

Mistakes happen. Big ones and small ones. The best way to move forward is to not get too bogged down by them; instead, try to use them as an opportunity to learn and improve. Because the truth is, if you want to be really good at something you have to be prepared to be really bad at it too. This is why people always recommend you try to do things you love, because it's a lot easier to bounce back when you are passionate about something. And afterwards you can spend time figuring out what went wrong and how you can do better next time.

I know that there will be one or two of you reading this, thinking, 'But Marcus, my dream was to be a footballer and I don't think I'll ever make it as a professional.'

Let me tell you, playing in front of 60,000 people every week isn't what makes you a football player. Kicking a ball about in the park and having fun — that's what makes you a footballer.

BE WILLING TO DREAM BIG AND FAIL BIG, BUT REMEMBER TO DO THINGS BECAUSE YOU LOVE TO DO THEM.

Denzel Washington is a famous and successful actor, who has made so many successful blockbuster films, but he always talks about how his true love is working in the theatre and doing small projects, just like in his school days.

And even when you do things you enjoy, be it football or acting, or dancing or photography, you have to understand that it will take time for you to get good at your craft. **BE HONEST WITH YOURSELF WHEN YOU MAKE A MISTAKE. TRY NOT TO POINT FINGERS AND BLAME OTHERS WHEN THINGS DON'T GO THE WAY YOU WANT.**

Be kind to yourself when mistakes happen as well. Understand that everything is part of a process, and bouncing back is just as important as moving forward. And always remember to be kind to others when they make mistakes too.

I've got one more quote from Denzel Washington I want to leave you with. It's actually something that his wife said to him, but it's a really important piece of advice that he still carries around with him:

TO GET SOMETHING YOU NEVER HAD, YOU HAVE TO DO SOMETHING YOU NEVER DID

It means that if you want to achieve amazing things, you will usually have to try something new in order to achieve it. You don't achieve great things by just doing the same things over and over. You have to challenge yourself and take risks. And taking risks often means that you are willing to make mistakes.

I know how lucky I am to be a professional footballer. I know that is a job that millions of people around the world dream of, but only a few get to do. I'll be honest with you though; it took thousands of hours for me to get to this point. It took loads of mistakes – small and large – for me to get to the place where I am now in my life. *I WAS WILLING TO 'FAIL BIG' AND LOSE, BUT I WAS NEVER PREPARED TO GIVE UP ON MYSELF.*

I'm also really lucky to have written books, which is another job many people around the world would like to do. You are reading the finished book now, but let me tell you, the pages you are reading took loads of different drafts, and many mistakes, big and small, before it got into your hands.

You are a lot more than any mistakes you have made in your life. Mistakes may happen in your future too, and I want you to know that they will not tell your full story either.

What matters most is the journey that you are on and the people you choose to connect with as you are on it.

I KNOW THAT LIFE CAN BE A STRUGGLE SOMETIMES, BUT SOME OF THE BEST THINGS IN LIFE COME AS CHALLENGES THAT YOU HAVE TO WORK THROUGH.

You can stumble, but make sure you never give up on yourself. If you do that, you might not always end up with a shiny trophy or an Oscar, but instead you will have loads of days where you go to bed with a smile on your face.

I PROMISE YOU THAT.

STORMZY

5

I WANT TO TALK TO YOU ABOUT A FRIEND OF MINE CALLED MICHAEL.

He's a brilliant musician. He's often on TV and the radio, and he does tons of live concerts too. Beyond that, he's a hugely charitable person who always tries to help as many people as possible.

You probably know him as Stormzy.

I first met Stormzy at a computer game event. I was with a few friends, and there was a competition to see who could be the best at this football game they had set up. You had to work in pairs — two vs two — so it wasn't enough to be good at the game by yourself. You also had to be a good teammate and communicate with the person you were paired with.

I'm really competitive, so I picked up one of the controllers and started playing along with my partner, trying to score goals and beat anyone we were up against.

We were doing pretty well, and then Stormzy came in with one of his friends and grabbed another controller. I want you to picture the four of us all playing this game in a packed room with everyone watching – Stormzy's competitive too, so our games got pretty hectic! I think both of us even shouted a few times because we were both so desperate to win.

The funny thing is, I can't remember who won that game. I DO remember that after we finished playing I introduced myself to Stormzy and told him I was a big fan of his music. I even showed him my phone where I had all his albums saved.

He told me he was a Manchester United fan and that he enjoyed watching me play. We had a brilliant night, and after that we became good friends. Whenever we're in the same city we always try to see each other, to talk and just hang out a bit (and play computer games!). I make an effort to see his shows whenever I have the time, and I always try to sneak backstage and see him afterwards.

Stormzy is one of the funniest, kindest people I know. You might not think it when you see him, but he gives some of the best hugs a friend could give you. He's one of the best friends you can have, because he's always trying to be the best version of himself.

He's also a great listener. Whenever we talk he always says:

He checks in on what's important to me.

What's more than that, if he says he's going to do something he will do it. And when you tell him that you want to do something, he will check up on you to make sure that you do it.

The way he sees it, we should all be trying to make our dreams happen. So if you tell Stormzy you're thinking of trying something new, he will do his best to help you.

A GOOD FRIEND IS A GOOD LISTENER, AND A GOOD LISTENER IS A GOOD LEARNER.

Stormzy is always trying to learn: how to be a better musician, how to be a better person, and how to help his friends to do better too.

And being his friend in turn helps me to become a better person.

A big reason why Stormzy is such a good friend comes from his upbringing. He grew up in a place in South London called Croydon. Now, Croydon is quite far from the centre of London. In fact, if you talk to someone who grew up in London they might tell you that Croydon isn't 'real London' or they might say it 'doesn't count'. It's a bit mean!

But what's great about Croydon is that the people who live there tend to make a special effort to look out for one another. If there's no help coming from the outside, they make sure there's loads of help inside Croydon.

It's difficult. Croydon isn't a perfect place to grow up, but the people from there care a lot about each other.

And Stormzy is one of them.

Stormzy's community in Croydon helped him to become the person he is now. He first started rapping and getting into music when he was eleven years old, in his local youth club. The whole club was run by locals who were volunteers and just wanted to help create a safer space where young people could hang out and express themselves.

When Stormzy was younger, he'd spend his time at the youth club writing lyrics and trying to rap, and other people in the club would give him tips on how to improve, and they'd also recommend other UK rappers he could listen to. Over time, thanks to the encouragement of his community, Stormzy began to get more confident in his style.

The thing about Stormzy is that he LOVES music. Throughout his life he's always been taking in all sorts of inspirations and influences to help him tell his stories. And the thing about growing up in South London is that there are plenty of things going on for him to take inspiration from. Stormzy raps about things like friendship, as well as his adventures in London and around the world. He raps about football, but also about how he loves his mum. He's proud of the area he's from, and he is really proud of how it helped make him the person he is today – *A BIT LIKE ME!*

That appreciation of his area, and how it came to influence him, carries through to everything Stormzy does. He still remembers all of those volunteers who helped him at the youth club, and he's always thinking of ways to give that positive experience to the next generation. The way he sees it, Michael wouldn't have become Stormzy if someone hadn't seen him writing lyrics and said,

TRY DOING IT THIS WAY INSTEAD.

So now, even though music is his first love, he's working to help the next generation find their own 'thing'. To find their dream, their passion, their hobby. That one thing a person will love that they will carry with them for the rest of their life!

Stormzy is a big advocate for helping people in that way. He wants to help ease the big stresses people can have in life, so they can put more energy into chasing their dreams.

That's why he does so many things outside of music to help people. Stormzy loves football, but he understands that it is not the easiest business to get into if you're not going to be a football player. That's why he set up a project – called Merky FC – which is all about getting more Black people into football. And the amazing thing is that it's not just about playing football (like I do), it's also about learning all of the different jobs available through the sport – things like how to be a football coach or sports presenter. Stormzy is passionate about getting more people into creative hobbies.

We both think that amazing things can happen when different people, people from all different backgrounds and walks of life, have the opportunity to work together.

Football is already amazing on the pitch because we have so many different players from all over the world who can come together and team up. So imagine how good it could be off the pitch too, with different coaches, different people on TV or different scouts?

There's more than one way to do something you love. You can love music, but you don't have to be a singer. You could be a producer, or a songwriter, or even work in stage production! There are loads of ways to express that passion. The best way to open doors and do what you're interested in is to learn as much as possible about it and then team up with other people who share your interest who can help you improve.

It's the idea of the youth club, just made much, much bigger!

To help with all of this, Stormzy has his own charity, called the #Merky Foundation, which has donated more than £500,000 to help fund college and university spaces for students from underprivileged backgrounds. He wants to help people learn as much as possible and make that learning as easy as possible.

He also set up the Stormzy Scholarship, which helps Black students get into some of the best universities in England for free each year too – that gives the opportunity for students to team up with loads of people who are interested in the same subjects as them.

On top of that, Stormzy is really interested in books, just like me! He has his own project, #Merky Books, which helps first-time writers get their ideas out of their imaginations and onto the page! #Merky Books has been really amazing with helping people to tell stories about people and places that you don't often hear about (like Croydon!). Stormzy also runs competitions to help new writers find their voice and tell their stories.

That's why I'm proud to be friends with Stormzy. He's one of the most unique, talented musicians I have ever met, but he's also honest and a hard worker. He understands that he wouldn't have got to the place where he is now without the hard work and opportunities that people before him opened up. So now he's working hard to give those opportunities to others. Even though music is his first love, he's not just working to look after the next generation of musicians. He's trying his hardest to help everyone find their thing. That's really inspiring. He is doing well, but he is always looking around to ensure the people around him are doing well too.

Stormzy and I get on so well because we both want to be out there, doing what we love and trying our best to look after the people around us. He's proud of Croydon just like I'm proud of Wythenshawe in Manchester, where I grew up.

I'm trying to help people in the same way people helped me in my local area when I was younger. I go back to my old primary school to help with writing competitions, a bit like how Stormzy runs #Merky Books.

I HOPE YOU, THE PERSON READING
THIS, CAN TAKE INSPIRATION FROM
YOUR LOCAL AREA.

THINK OF WHAT YOU LIKE ABOUT IT
AND HOW IT'S HELPED MAKE YOU
WHO YOU ARE TODAY.

THINK OF HOW YOU CAN TAKE THOSE
LESSONS AND PASS THEM ON
TO PEOPLE AROUND YOU.

I'll give you a really quick example. When I was growing up all of the kids in Wythenshawe would ride their bikes to get around the place. We'd go to the local park, have races and do as much as possible on our bikes. Kids in Wythenshawe are really good at riding bikes, but our love of cycling means that we're also really good at fixing bikes when something goes wrong (and things would often go wrong with them!).

Growing up around all of that, means I'm still pretty good with bikes to this day. I'm a good cyclist, but I can also help fix my mates' bikes if something is off. On top of that, I really care about making cycling safer in Manchester too!

Have a think about the hobbies that you picked up growing up in your area. I bet if someone asked you how to get more people into your favourite hobby, you'd have a few ideas. Why don't you try putting those ideas into practice?

Look at Stormzy — he's helped show the world that there's more than one way to chase your dreams. He's also shown the world that there are so many ways you can help your friends chase theirs.

Do you have a friend who is interested in music, just like Stormzy?

Why don't you offer to listen to some of their music?

Do you have a friend who is really into art?

Ask them to make something for you and see what they say!

Got a friend who is into cycling or skateboarding?

Try to go to the skate park with them and see what makes them so happy!

REMEMBER: THE BEST WAY TO OPEN DOORS FOR OTHER PEOPLE AND DO WHAT YOU'RE INTERESTED IN IS TO LEARN AS MUCH AS YOU CAN ABOUT IT. THEN YOU CAN TEAM UP WITH PEOPLE WHO SHARE YOUR INTEREST, AND YOU CAN HELP EACH OTHER IMPROVE.

A GOOD FRIEND IS A GOOD
LISTENER, AND A GOOD LISTENER
IS A GOOD LEARNER. I WANT YOU TO
THINK OF HOW YOU CAN BE A
GOOD LISTENER TO YOUR FRIENDS.

THINK OF WHAT YOU CAN LEARN ABOUT
THEM AND HOW YOU CAN HELP THEM BE THE
BEST THEY CAN BE. AND TOGETHER, BY
SHARING YOUR PASSIONS, YOU'LL FIND
THERE'S SO MANY DIFFERENT WAYS
TO DO WHAT YOU LOVE.

SERENA WILLIAMS

6

THERE AREN'T MANY PEOPLE IN THE WORLD LIKE
SERENA WILLIAMS. SHE IS, WITHOUT A DOUBT, ONE OF
THE GREATEST TENNIS PLAYERS OF ALL TIME. AND
BEYOND THAT, SHE IS A TRAILBLAZER FOR BLACK
WOMEN IN SPORTS.

Back in school, I used to play a bit of tennis. It didn't matter whether
it was singles or doubles, I just loved to play. Even now I
try to watch the big tournaments whenever I can. There's
something about the mental side of tennis that I find really
interesting. The way that the top players are able to hold their
nerve on the big points is amazing!

Tennis has a really focused, competitive edge to it; when you're out there on the court, you're on your own. You have to block out the noise from the crowd, stop paying attention to the scoreboard and just focus on the task at hand.

Over the years, I've watched a lot of Serena Williams' tennis matches, and let me tell you, she's one of the best to ever pick up a racket. Her achievements speak for themselves. Serena has won twenty-three grand slams over the course of her career, including seven singles titles at Wimbledon. She's won four gold medals at the Olympics too. Serena was once number one in the women's rankings for 186 weeks in a row. That means for **THREE AND A HALF YEARS** no one was better at tennis than her.

That's not even the only time she was ranked number one. In total, Serena Williams was ranked number one in the world for a total of 319 weeks.

THERE'S GREATNESS, **AND THEN** **THERE'S SERENA.** SHE WAS ON A DIFFERENT LEVEL FOR SO LONG.

She was the best – week in and week out – in a sport that demands a lot from you, both physically and mentally.

You can't just play better than the person on the other side of the court; you have to make sure you are *thinking* better than them too. A lot of people compare the mental element of tennis with boxing. There's no punching involved in tennis, but you have to have the same appreciation for footwork and technique in everything you do. Speed is really important when you're playing tennis too – a lot of the best tennis players can hit shots that go faster than seventy miles per hour. That can be faster than the blink of an eye! Imagine that; to be a good tennis player you have to think *and* react *and* return a shot in the time it takes most people to blink!

Then remember that a lot of tennis matches can take many hours to complete. It's a fun sport, but to become really good at it you need to put in a lot of time, training and sacrifice.

Serena Williams put in the hard work and dedication to be at the top of her game for nearly twenty years. But one of the things that I find most

incredible about Serena is her journey to get to the top: she could never have reached those heights without help from her friends and family.

When Serena was really young her family moved to a place called Compton, California, in the USA. Serena was the youngest daughter in the family and was really close to her older sister, Venus. Their dad, Richard Williams, started teaching Serena and Venus how to play tennis when they were just four and six years old.

Richard Williams used to home-school Serena and Venus, making sure they had a good education but also making sure that they had enough time each day to play tennis against each other. By the time Serena was nine, the family had moved again to train under a tennis coach called Rick Macci, and people thought Serena was one of the best Under-10 tennis players in the country.

The thing is, even though people *thought* that Serena was one of the best players, they wouldn't always *say* it. Back in the 1990s, when Serena was starting her career, there weren't many Black people in the world playing tennis professionally. It was considered to be a sport that was mostly for people who had a lot of money and didn't live in the inner cities, in areas like Compton in the USA (or Manchester, where I'm from in the UK). So even though Serena and Venus would go to tournaments and clearly be the best young players around, many parents and tennis coaches didn't want to admit it. There were a lot of racist and close-minded people who thought Venus and Serena were lying about their ages so they could play in Under-10 competitions. Both Williams girls were called cheats when they won tournaments. Or even worse.

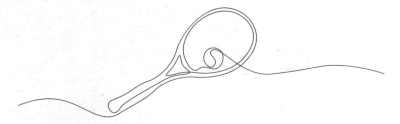

Eventually, things got so bad that when Serena was fourteen Richard decided to take both Serena and Venus out of Macci's coaching school so he could focus on their training at home. The way he saw it, the tennis world wasn't ready to properly protect his family, so he had to teach both his daughters Serena and Venus how to look after each other instead.

I think about this a lot. Everyone in the tennis world knew how good the Williams sisters were when they were only nine and eleven years old, but no one wanted to look after them or make tennis safer for two Black kids. So rather than wait and hope the tennis world would one day accept them, both Williams girls set about pushing each other and changing the world with their talents.

That takes a tremendous amount of mental strength as well as skill. That's also why both Serena and Venus are so good at what they do: a good tennis player can block out the noise of the crowd, but a great tennis player, like Serena, can do things that completely changed what the people in the crowd thought was possible. Serena and Venus were able to push themselves to be the best that they could be, because they had their father, and they had each other.

Serena played in a very important tennis match in 2001. In this match she was playing against Venus in the final of the US Open. It was the first time since 1884 that two siblings had played each other in a major tennis final, and there was a lot of noise about it. Everyone wanted to know which of the two sisters would win.

Venus ended up winning that match, but afterwards, she gave her younger sister a massive hug, and Serena admitted that she had felt nervous facing her sister in front of so many people. It was an amazing moment to watch.

Loads of people in the crowd felt that competition between the two sisters had to come with nastiness, but Serena and Venus proved that there was a bond between the two of them that the competition couldn't break. *THEY WERE BEST FRIENDS, EVEN THOUGH THEY WERE COMPETING AGAINST EACH OTHER.*

There's no jealousy
between the two.
They love each other and
both know, better than anyone, the hard work
and training they've each put into the sport. So rather
than pay attention to what everyone is saying on the
outside, they focus on what really matters: protecting each
other, pushing each other, and being there for each other.

Serena would end up playing Venus a lot at Wimbledon. Those matches
were always intense, but you also got to see the love they have for
each other. I've watched a lot of those matches on YouTube, and what's
amazing is how both sisters get really annoyed at themselves after
losing points. But then, immediately after, they'll crack a smile because
they realise how fun it is to do the thing they love with their best friend.

Over time, Serena overcame her nerves and started to beat Venus
regularly, but together they helped change the face of tennis. Serena
has seven Wimbledon titles and Venus has five.

What's more, Serena and Venus didn't just play against each other in singles competitions, but they would also play *next to each other* in doubles competitions too. Three of Serena's Olympic gold medals have come from playing tennis with her sister. I think that is just great.

Serena has said that she wouldn't have become the great tennis player she is known to be around the world if it hadn't been for Venus. They were there, together, day after day, pushing each other to be the best they can possibly be. They challenged each other every step of the way, and together they are two of the greatest tennis players of all time.

I've got a fun fact for you. Did you know that many professional athletes are younger siblings? No one is completely sure why, but I think it has a lot to do with all of the games you play as a child. If you have an older sibling you might understand. Is there a game that you play a lot with your siblings? It could be a sport, a board game, or some other challenge! When you play against each other does your older sibling tend to beat you? If so, don't be disheartened! *WHAT THEY ARE DOING IS HELPING YOU TO TRAIN TO BECOME THE BEST VERSION OF YOURSELF.*

THEY SAY THAT THE YOUNGER SIBLING OFTEN TURNS OUT TO BE THE BEST ATHLETE BECAUSE THEY LEARN HOW TO IMPROVE THEIR GAME BY PLAYING AGAINST SOMEONE BIGGER AND OLDER THAN THEM EVERY DAY.

This means that when they go to school, join another team and face people in their age group, they don't get too worried about facing people closer to their age.

Serena spent every single day playing against her sister, who was two years older than her. Venus was faster and stronger than her growing up, so Serena learned from a very young age how to think quicker than her sister in order to make shots.

You probably already know that I have two older brothers, Dwaine and Dane. The age gap between us is pretty big, but both of them used to take me to the park to play football against the older kids. I think that playing against my brothers and their friends really helped me growing up. I had to work on my technique to compete against them when I was ten, but by the time I was fourteen my brothers admitted I was so good at football that they didn't want to play with me any more!

So if you're reading this right now and you have an older sibling who beats you at a game, don't get too angry — they're training you to one day be the best at it! Trust me.

YOU MIGHT NOT SEE THE IMPROVEMENTS DAY-BY-DAY, BUT WHEN YOU LOOK BACK AFTERWARDS, YOU'LL BE ABLE TO SEE IT CLEARLY.

If you're reading this and you don't have an older sibling, I don't want you to get too worried. I believe that you have the family you are related to, and then the family you choose. I think of many of my friends as my chosen family, and I know that my friends have pushed me to be the best that I can be just as much as my siblings have.

And if you're reading this and ***you*** are the older sibling . . . just know that you won't be on top for too long! Haha! I'm only joking! Being older doesn't mean you're going to be bad at sport – look at Venus Williams, she's an amazing tennis player in her own right! I think it's great whenever a person has someone to play games with, no matter who wins.

THE TIME THAT YOU SPEND WITH THE PEOPLE YOU LOVE IS JUST AS IMPORTANT AS ALL OF THE SKILLS YOU LEARN.

There are so many reasons why Serena is an inspiration to me. She and her family helped to change tennis for the better – nowadays there are more Black people playing tennis than ever before, and the Williams family helped to make this possible.

More than that, Serena and Venus Williams remind me every day of the importance of my own family – and by that I don't just mean my blood relatives, like my mum, my brothers and my sisters, but I also mean my friends. The people who I have *chosen* to be my family.

To me, family is a bond that is held between people who love and care for each other. You don't need to look the same, or have the same surname, to care for another person. I like to think that your journey will bring people into your life who you might come to see as family.

The love and support of my family and friends has helped me to become the person I am today. They've pushed me to be the best version of myself that I can be. I know that you have people around you who want you to be the best you can possibly be too. It might be a parent, a sibling, a teacher, a coach or a friend, but I promise you there are *always* people who are on your team, even when you might not feel like they are.

I promise you that I will always be on your team, and I want you to remember that the people around you are important, so find the ones who lift you up and hold on to them. Look out for them, and protect them.

Try to remember that it's important to be that person for others as well. There will always be someone out there who wants you to be the best version of yourself that you can be, in the same way Richard Williams wanted what was best for Serena and Venus. In the same way that Venus and Serena have always wanted what's best for each other. What's important is recognising who those people are, and learning to trust and give that love back in kind.

REMEMBER

THAT A BIT OF FRIENDLY COMPETITION CAN BE FUN, AND CAN HELP YOU AND YOUR FAMILY TO PUSH EACH OTHER AND HELP EACH OTHER. BUT REMEMBER, ABOVE ALL, THAT YOU ARE ONLY IN COMPETITION WITH YOURSELF.

The Williams sisters are champions not just because of their sporting skills, but because when the world was harsh to them they chose to protect each other. You can do this with your family, friends and teammates too. You can all be champions by showing the people closest to you that you care about them and you appreciate what they bring to your life.

I always try to keep my friends and my family at the centre of everything I do, and I remind myself that I wouldn't be where I am today without the people around me. Life can be hard sometimes and you don't always get what you want, but if you try to spend as many days as you can with the people who understand you best, you'll be surprised at the amount of good things that can happen.

SIR ALEX FERGUSON

7

SIR ALEX FERGUSON IS THE LEGENDARY FORMER MANAGER OF MANCHESTER UNITED. He is widely considered to be one of the greatest football managers of all time. In fact, when I was born, in 1997, people already thought he was one of the best football managers in the country. He'd been Manchester United's manager for eleven years at that point, and he still had another sixteen years left in his career!

Twenty-six years. That's how long Sir Alex was at the top of his profession. That's how long he was doing brilliant things for the football club I love.

Between 1986 and 2013, Sir Alex would win an incredible thirty-eight trophies for the club. Under his leadership Manchester United won the Premier League thirteen times, the FA Cup five times and the UEFA Champions League twice. In 1999 Sir Alex led United to what is known as the 'Treble' – where they won the Premier League, FA Cup and Champions League all in the same season. Very few football teams in Europe have ever won a Treble – to do so means you are the best of the very best in any given season! Under Sir Alex, Manchester United were the first ever club in England to do that. Not long after winning the Treble, Sir Alex was knighted by Queen Elizabeth II for his contribution to the sport.

I was nine when I first met Sir Alex, and I already knew all about his incredible achievements. Manchester United were the best football team in England at this point. I was already a footballer for United and I would go down to their training ground – called The Cliff – to work on my skills. There was a little balcony just above the gym where I would stand and watch the senior players work with Sir Alex's coaching staff. Sometimes, if my Under-10 or Under-12 team was training later in the day, I might catch a glimpse of the grown-ups on the pitch. It was an incredible learning experience; I would try my best to soak up all the information around me, watching how the adults trained and listening hard to what Sir Alex and the other coaches wanted from them, so I could try to apply that in my training with the youth team. He's always been a huge inspiration to me.

I WAS ONLY YOUNG, BUT IT WAS CLEAR EVEN AT THAT POINT THAT SIR ALEX WAS **BRILLIANT AT MOTIVATING PLAYERS** AND GETTING THEM TO **GIVE THEIR ALL FOR THE CAUSE.**

Training sessions at United can be difficult; if you want to be the best football team in the country you need to have the fittest, most skilled and most dedicated players.

It can be hard to give 100 per cent every day and all of the time, but Sir Alex and his coaching staff had a way of making sure players reached their peak at the right time so that they could win the most important games.

Sir Alex was also brilliant at man-management, and he would go out of his way to remember little bits about every single player. Things like how they liked their cups of tea, whether they were an early riser or a night owl, or their favourite snacks.

Sir Alex would keep notes on how many languages players spoke, because at a club as big as United there were moments when players would need help translating ideas. If someone came in who couldn't speak great English, but could speak French, Sir Alex would pair them up with someone from France to help them get comfortable. He knew which players were really competitive and which ones needed a bit of extra motivation when things got tough. He was a clear communicator too; if he was going to pick one player over another for a big game, he'd sit them both down and tell them the reasons why. He was fair.

Sir Alex Ferguson was a great leader, not just because he won loads of games and tons of trophies for Manchester United. He was a great leader because he worked hard to understand people. He knew how to get a collection of individuals to come together and, most importantly, he knew how to get those individuals to work like a team. Sir Alex was never just focused on one person – he knew that it wasn't just star players that would make a club great, but the way that all the players came together as a team. The team was always his focus. How to make them the best in the country and how to stay the best, year in and year out.

SIR ALEX WAS A BRILLIANT MANAGER BECAUSE HE REALISED THE BEST TEAM WASN'T JUST THE BEST ELEVEN PLAYERS PUT TOGETHER. HE UNDERSTOOD THAT A TEAM HAD TO HAVE A CERTAIN FIT – YOU HAD TO MAKE SURE A TEAM HAD COMBINATIONS THAT WORKED TOGETHER AND BROUGHT THE BEST OUT OF EVERYONE.

When I was younger, my favourite Manchester United defender was Rio Ferdinand. He was really quick and good at passing the ball. Sir Alex used to put him next to a defender called Nemanja Vidić, who was REALLY strong and loved making tackles. On their own, each defender was really good, but when they worked together they were almost unstoppable!

That's Sir Alex's skill. He'd bring you into the team, figure out how you worked and what you were good at, and then he'd pair you with someone who matched up well with your skills. Someone who could bring the best out of you. **_HE UNDERSTOOD THAT PEOPLE ARE STRONGER WHEN THEY WORK TOGETHER_**. Even now, when I play football, I'm not the best striker, so my managers often play me next to players who can help me focus on what I'm good at, so that in turn I can use my talents to help make them even better.

The first time I met Sir Alex I was having lunch in the canteen at Manchester United's training ground. He came over to say hello to me and some of the other children in the team's academy. We were all completely awestruck. Sir Alex sat down at the table where all of us kids were sitting and said, 'If you go and work hard, one day you could be there', before pointing at a table where all the first-team players were getting their food.

The fact that he made the effort to come and talk to us kids made us all feel special. What we wanted more than anything in the world was to be a part of the senior team one day, and Sir Alex made us feel that he believed in us. It was things like that which made him a great motivator. He was telling us that if we worked hard enough, we could achieve our dreams. He was a manager who was supposed to spend all of his time taking care of the senior team players – proper grown-ups – but he was using his lunchtime to make sure a bunch of under-10s were OK. I wouldn't play for United's senior team for another nine years, after Sir Alex had retired, but here he was making sure I knew that I was part of the club's plans for the future.

That evening I went home and told my older brother Dwaine what had happened at lunchtime. Dwaine told me that it was really cool that Sir Alex was looking out for me because he was a football manager with a reputation for trusting young players. Some football managers prefer more experienced players in big games, but Sir Alex always used to say:

'IF YOU'RE GOOD ENOUGH, THEN YOU'RE OLD ENOUGH.'

Age was never a barrier for Sir Alex. Hard work and talent were all that mattered. He would give playing opportunities to players of all ages, so long as he believed in them. And he inspired players to work hard and be the best they could be in training and during matches too.

A good leader makes sure that everyone in their team knows they are important, and that everyone knows they have a role to play. Sir Alex was really great at that.

It's something that I try to take forward when I'm around my friends and family too. I try to remember the little things about people, and champion their success wherever possible. I want to make sure I make time for everyone around me, to show them that I care about them and that I believe in them. Remember that talking to the people around you, whether it's a teammate, a sibling or a classmate, can really make a difference to them. Show the people around you that you care about them – check in with them, ask them how they are or what they're enjoying right now.

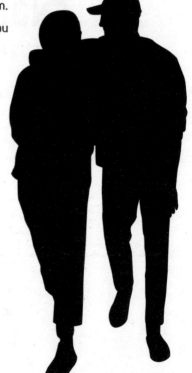

THINK ABOUT ALL OF
THE THINGS YOU KNOW ABOUT
YOUR BEST FRIEND. YOU PROBABLY
ALREADY KNOW WHAT THEIR FAVOURITE
FOOD IS, OR WHAT SORT OF HOBBIES THEY
HAVE, BUT WHEN WAS THE LAST TIME THEY
TOLD YOU ABOUT THEIR AMBITIONS?

DO YOU THINK YOU CAN HELP THEM
TO REACH THEIR DREAMS?

It's important to think about your family and your friends as your own team, and to think about little things you can do to help your team work better together. Do something nice for them, even if it's something as simple as a smile or a hug – you never know how that might change someone's day for the better.

I want you to think about how you can bring people with different skills together. You're so much stronger in a team than you are on your own, and by working together you can do amazing things, whether it's helping each other to get better at a subject at school, or working together on something creatively, like a piece of music. Remember that brilliant things can happen when you bring together different ideas and different perspectives – the best teams work well when different people come together and help each other while you all work towards the same goal.

ABOVE ALL,

TRY YOUR BEST

TO FIND WAYS TO

HELP YOUR TEAMMATES.

**THE IMPORTANT THING
ABOUT A TEAM IS THAT**

EVERYONE FEELS WELCOME,

EVERYONE HAS A PLACE,

AND

EVERYONE FEELS VALUED.

I try to be like Sir Alex every day. Not because I want to win loads of things for Manchester United (although I do!), but because I like putting together winning teams. I like to think of my family as a winning team, especially when my mum is happy, or when my brothers and sisters have good news. Manchester United is a winning team, and so are my group of best friends away from football.

I like to think you – yes you! The one reading this book! – are on a winning team too! And I want you to know that when you read this book, you're part of a collection of people who are all trying to do brilliant things with their lives. So let's try to be good teammates and help each other wherever possible.

MUHAMMAD ALI

8

HAVE YOU EVER PLAYED THAT GAME WHERE YOU ASK YOUR FRIENDS WHO THEIR THREE IDEAL DINNER GUESTS WOULD BE? Sometimes you can choose fictional characters, and sometimes you choose real people (it's a fun game, so if you haven't played it I would recommend you try it!).

Not too long ago, someone asked me to pick the three people from anywhere in history I'd like to have dinner with. I thought about it for a little while before I answered:

DENZEL WASHINGTON

BARACK OBAMA

MUHAMMAD ALI

You might already know of Barack Obama — he was the first Black President of the United States and has done SO much cool stuff! — and I've already told you why I think Denzel Washington is great. For now, I want to talk to you about Muhammad Ali.

Muhammad Ali is also known as 'The Greatest'. Throughout history there have been many athletes who have been referred to as 'The Greatest', and I'm sure that some of you reading this might be familiar with the term *'THE G.O.A.T.' — THE GREATEST OF ALL TIME*.

But if you ask any athlete to talk about the greatest ever athlete, and I mean the **GREATEST EVER**, they will probably talk about Muhammad Ali.

It doesn't matter where in the world they come from. It doesn't matter what sport they play. **Everyone** knows that Muhammad Ali is one of the most important people to ever play sports. Everyone understands why he used to call himself 'The Greatest', and everyone agrees that he paved the way for so many people who came after him.

Not just in boxing but in **all sports.**

Let me explain. You may already know that when I was younger I'd spend a lot of my time watching sports highlights on YouTube. And it wasn't just football – I'd watch basketball, tennis, boxing, all types of sports. I wanted to learn as much as I could about as many sports as possible. I was one of those kids who liked learning about world records: finding out who was the fastest, who was the strongest, or who had won the most titles in their sport. Then, one day, I stumbled across a video of Muhammad Ali boxing in the 1970s.

It was *incredible*.

Boxing is a very dangerous sport, but Ali made it look beautiful. The way he moved in the ring was out of this world. There's this famous quote that one of his coaches once said to him, which perfectly described his boxing style:

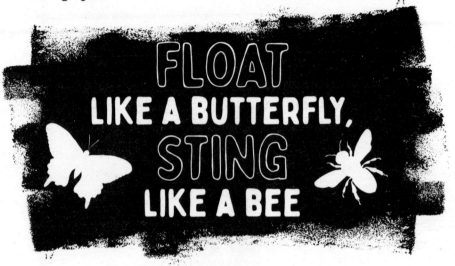

FLOAT
LIKE A BUTTERFLY,
STING
LIKE A BEE

And he really did float like a butterfly. His footwork was excellent. It was like he was dancing in the ring.

And then. **Bang**.

Bang.

Bang.

Ali's punches were so fast that it was hard to keep track of where his hands were. Before you knew it, his matches were over. He was tall, he was fast, he had great strength, and he was really intelligent with how he used his talents. Ali won fifty-six boxing matches throughout his career. Two of those wins are considered the greatest boxing matches of all time.

The first was called the *Rumble in the Jungle*, which took place in 1974. There, Ali fought a much bigger and much stronger opponent called George Foreman, and he used this special tactic called the 'Rope-A-Dope' to defeat him. The Rope-A-Dope was a really clever play where Ali spent much of the bout resting on the ropes of the boxing ring, blocking Foreman's punches while waiting for him to tire himself out. Foreman was really strong but not used to his matches lasting too long. So when Foreman got tired from all the punching, Ali, who was still feeling fresh, managed to defeat him. It's still considered to be one of the biggest boxing upsets of all time!

Ali also won a famous boxing match in 1975 called the *Thrilla in Manila*. This was against a boxer called Joe Frazier. This match is really famous because at the time they were the two best boxers in the world.

Boxing isn't for everyone (it can be dangerous!), but many people — even those who don't like the sport — agree that those matches were very important events.

Muhammad Ali was the first fighter to win the world heavyweight championship three times. He was also confident. He used to talk a lot about why he was brilliant (which I'll admit might make him sound arrogant and sometimes made people angry!), but he could always back it up. He knew that his hard work and dedicated training meant that he would be able to deliver on his promises, even when things got hard.

But there's more to him than what he did inside the ring – ***BEING ONE OF THE GREATEST BOXERS EVER IS ONLY PART OF HIS STORY.***

You see, Ali's life was about more than just sporting excellence. *ALI IS AN ICON TO MANY PEOPLE BECAUSE HIS STORY IS ABOUT WORKING HARD AND STANDING UP FOR WHAT YOU BELIEVE IN, EVEN WHEN THE ODDS ARE AGAINST YOU.*

Ali grew up in Louisville in the USA. One day, when Ali was only twelve years old, someone stole his bicycle. He was going up and down the streets of Louisville asking everyone he met if they had seen who had taken his bike. (When I was twelve I loved my bike, so I can imagine how upset he would have been when someone stole it!)

While he was looking for his bike he bumped into a policeman by a boxing gym. The policeman suggested that Ali learn how to box, as a new hobby, while he tried to find his bike. Can you imagine that? One of the greatest sportspeople of all time only got into their sport after losing their bike. One of the best things to happen to boxing, and to sport as a whole, happened because someone had a really low moment when they were twelve years old.

I THINK ABOUT THAT
A LOT. YOU NEVER KNOW WHICH
EVENTS HAVE TO HAPPEN TO UNLOCK YOUR
TRUE GREATNESS. SOMETIMES IT CAN BE A
SPECIAL, BRILLIANT MOMENT. SOMETIMES IT CAN
BE SOMETHING REALLY ANNOYING OR UPSETTING,
LIKE LOSING YOUR BIKE. BUT ALL OF THESE EVENTS
ARE IMPORTANT IN YOUR LIFE, AS THEY HELP
TO SHAPE YOU INTO THE PERSON YOU ARE.

ALI GOT INTO BOXING BECAUSE HE WANTED
TO BE ABLE TO STAND UP FOR HIMSELF.
BUT HE BECAME 'THE GREATEST' BECAUSE
HE WANTED TO USE BOXING AS A WAY
TO STAND UP FOR EVERYONE.

As well as a boxer, Ali was an amazing public speaker and campaigner. Throughout his life, he would donate millions of dollars to various charities and organisations, as well as run multiple campaigns to try and help people around the world. It's estimated that Ali has helped feed more than 22 MILLION people worldwide! That's enough people to fill a country!

If you've watched any videos of Ali online, you've probably noticed that he talks a lot. He had this cool style of talking that sounded like poetry because of all the rhymes and jokes he would put in. But there was always this weight behind what he was saying. He would never say something just for the effect. There's a lot of sense and truth to the words that would flow off his tongue.

IF HE SAID HE WAS THE BEST BOXER IN THE WORLD, HE MEANT IT.

IF HE SAID HE THOUGHT IT WAS IMPORTANT FOR YOUNG PEOPLE TO ATTEND UNIVERSITY, HE'D HELP AND SUPPORT CHARITIES TO GET MORE PEOPLE THERE.

He once said that,

SERVICE TO OTHERS IS THE RENT YOU PAY FOR YOUR ROOM HERE ON EARTH

I think that is just the most amazing idea. Ali thought that every person was carrying a gift. That we all have these talents and whilst we are all on our journeys of growth and development, we should never get so focused on taking care of ourselves that we forget to take care of other people. Yes, we're all humans trying to go about our day and be the best that we can be, but to Ali – and to me – *THE MOST IMPORTANT THING THAT YOU CAN DO WITH YOUR TIME IS TO TRY YOUR BEST TO HELP OTHERS.*

Ali may have been a boxer, but he used to talk about the importance of peace as well. In 1966 Ali was called up to join the US Army and fight in the Vietnam War, but he refused.

THE VIETNAM WAR WAS A CONFLICT BETWEEN THE UNITED STATES AND VIETNAM, A COUNTRY IN SOUTH-EAST ASIA. IT WAS A WAR THAT STARTED A LOT OF DISCUSSION AROUND THE WORLD AS MANY PEOPLE THOUGHT IT COULD HAVE BEEN AVOIDED WITH PEOPLE TALKING TO EACH OTHER, RATHER THAN FIGHTING.

Ali's decision not to join the army caused a lot of controversy at the time; Ali was the heavyweight champion of the world and one of the most well-known people in the United States, but he publicly said that he believed that his country going to war was a bad idea.

Many people were angry at him for what he said and wanted him to apologise. But Ali stood firm in his beliefs, even when the government got involved and took him to court. Eventually, he was stripped of his boxing titles and sent to jail.

Ali stood up for what he believed in. He was a boxer, yes, but he believed that war was wrong and he didn't want to fight in Vietnam. And even when he was punished for standing up for what he believed in, he stood firm. He wouldn't box for three years after being stripped of the title, and he became an anti-war protester. He was a very important figure for the communities he was standing up for.

ALI CHOSE PEACE INSTEAD OF WAR AT GREAT PERSONAL COST. But by using his platform to speak out, he was able to show people in the United States how much he believed war was wrong. This, in turn, inspired many more people to speak out against the war.

Muhammad Ali is one of the greatest boxers of all time, but the greatest fight he had was one he *didn't win*. He showed the world the value of *inner* strength. That even though doing the right thing can sometimes be a difficult route to take, it's important you do it and stand up for what you believe in.

It's a lesson I think about nearly every single day. Doing the right thing sometimes means going through tough moments in your life.

DOING THE RIGHT THING DOESN'T ALWAYS MEAN DOING THE EASY THING.

BUT THOSE DIFFICULT MOMENTS ARE IMPORTANT, NOT JUST FOR YOU BUT ALSO FOR THE PEOPLE AROUND YOU.

In 2020 I played a game for England against Belgium, and I wore a special pair of boots. Written along the sides was a quote from Muhammad Ali. It read,

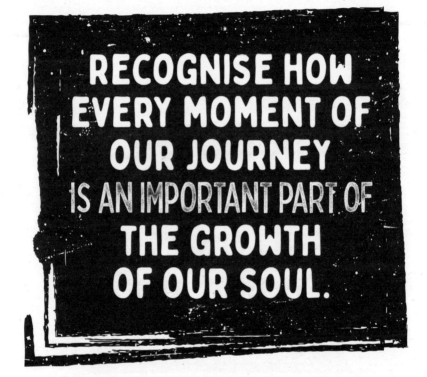

RECOGNISE HOW EVERY MOMENT OF OUR JOURNEY IS AN IMPORTANT PART OF THE GROWTH OF OUR SOUL.

It's one of my favourite quotes ever. It means that Ali thought that everything that happened to him, from the high point of winning the title to the low points of going to prison and losing his title, helped to make him a better person. The quote reminds me that the difficult moments in our life can be as important as the good moments, because all your experience helps to shape who you are as a person.

I think the biggest thing that I've taken from Muhammad Ali was the way he held firm in his beliefs. Ali knew the way he talked and the way he acted would rub some people up the wrong way, but also he knew that helping people and staying true to his beliefs was more important than any criticism that might come his way. He once said,

I DON'T HAVE TO BE WHO YOU WANT ME TO BE. I'M FREE TO BE WHO I WANT.

I try to be like that in my life. When I was a kid, I never tried to act a certain way to get into a specific friendship group in school or my area. I tried to do the right thing wherever possible. I still do. If I believe something's wrong and I feel strongly enough to speak about it, I will try my best to do so. That's why I have campaigned against homelessness in the past, and why I asked so many of you to help me in my anti-food poverty campaigns too.

I know that speaking out and standing up for what I think is important isn't going to make everyone happy, but I think it's important to listen to people in need and try your best to help them whenever possible. *It doesn't mean I'll get it right every time, but that's alright.*

THE ONLY WAY YOU CAN TRULY FAIL IS BY GIVING UP.

I HOPE THAT ONE DAY, PEOPLE WILL KNOW THAT I TRIED MY BEST TO STAND UP FOR WHAT I BELIEVED IN AND THAT I LOOKED TO HELP OTHERS WHEREVER POSSIBLE.

I hope that talking a bit about Muhammad Ali has helped to inspire you in your life too. Remember how important it is to find out what you feel passionate about and to stand up for what you believe in — for yourself and your own life, but also for other people in the world around you. I'm not asking you to become one of the best boxers of all time (although I'm sure you could if you wanted to!) but I would like you to think about the things that you believe in most, and how you might be able to help the community around you.

Do you care about the environment? Maybe you can join a campaign to stand up for local wildlife! Or if you like reading, you can make sure to join your local library and support them by borrowing lots of books. Standing up for what you believe in can come in all shapes and sizes – even small actions can help to make the world a better place, and when you're contributing to something you care passionately about, you'll find it easier to do the right thing, even when it might not be the easiest route you can take.

Ali was a brilliant boxer, but he's called The Greatest because he talked about the importance of peace and helping one another. He was physically strong, but he knew that true strength came from being kind and helping people. He knew that true strength came from doing the right thing, no matter what, even when people try to shut you down. The most powerful thing you can do in this life is to reach out to another person and offer them help in their time of need.

When Ali passed away in 2016 he left behind the most amazing legacy. Muhammad Ali called himself 'The Greatest', and we all agreed.

HE WAS THE GREATEST. HE WAS A SPECIAL ATHLETE AND AN EXCEPTIONAL HUMAN BEING.

Ali was known for what he did in the ring with a closed fist, but the most important thing he taught us was how it was crucial we open our hands and our hearts to other people, and stand up for what we think is right. There will be good times and bad in your journey. But I want you to remember that, like Ali said,

EVERY MOMENT IS IMPORTANT IN OUR GROWTH

MELANIE MAYNARD

9

I WANT TO TELL YOU A LITTLE BIT ABOUT MY MUM.

When I was growing up my mum worked two jobs a lot of the time in order to support our family. She was the only adult in the house, so things were often tough.

My mum was working all of the time, week in and week out, to make sure there was food on the table and enough money to pay the bills. She did everything she could to make sure her five children had all they needed; she wanted us to be ready to go out into the wider world and be safe and confident.

She was out of the house a lot because she was always working. But when she was in, she was 100 per cent there for all of us: listening to our stories about how we got on at school, giving us advice and making sure we weren't getting into trouble with anyone.

If I needed something for school, she would make sure I had it. But beyond that she made sure to teach me important life lessons, so that I knew things like to be careful on the walk back after school, and to take care of myself when I was outside with friends. My mum would even speak to people who lived and worked in the local area so that they would look after me when I was out playing football if she was away at work. Just so she knew that someone was looking out for me when she wasn't there.

And that was just me. My mum was doing all of this for my brothers and sisters too. She made sure all of her children were looked after.

There were some nights growing up when my mum literally wouldn't sleep because she'd have to do back-to-back shifts at work. She'd have her main job in town during the day, and then she'd go straight to a cleaning job in the evening after that. Her second 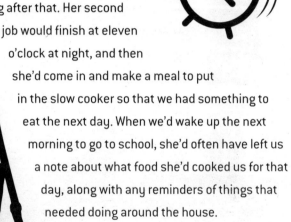 job would finish at eleven o'clock at night, and then she'd come in and make a meal to put in the slow cooker so that we had something to eat the next day. When we'd wake up the next morning to go to school, she'd often have left us a note about what food she'd cooked us for that day, along with any reminders of things that needed doing around the house.

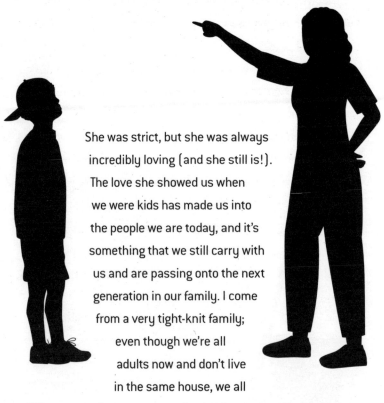

She was strict, but she was always incredibly loving (and she still is!). The love she showed us when we were kids has made us into the people we are today, and it's something that we still carry with us and are passing onto the next generation in our family. I come from a very tight-knit family; even though we're all adults now and don't live in the same house, we all still live pretty close to one another in Manchester. We bicker from time to time — as all families do — but when it comes down to it everyone looks out for one another. We all support each other as best as we can. That's something that we got from our mum.

Whenever I talk to my mum I always try to remind her of the unbelievable job she's done raising all five of her children. And beyond that, I want her to know the impact she's had on her friends in the area she lives in. She's been a pillar of strength to her local community too, inspiring all those around her. She has a kindness that's really infectious.

Growing up, my mum was the busiest person you have ever met. Like I said there were days when she literally didn't have time to eat dinner or sleep properly. She knew that it was important to look after herself, but she always made time to make sure that she was kind to other people. If she could help someone, she would.

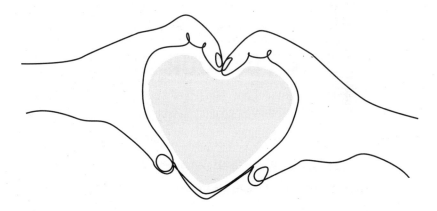

This one time I saw my mum cut her lunch break short at work because someone had asked her for directions. She could have just said, 'Sorry I'm busy', and taken her full break, but she decided to help this person who was lost and in need of help.

She was always teaching us life lessons in that way.

IF YOU CAN HELP SOMEONE IN THE NEXT FIVE MINUTES, WHY NOT DO IT? IF IT DOESN'T TAKE MUCH OF YOUR TIME, WHY NOT HELP SOMEONE?

That's my mum: Melanie Maynard. Nearly everything I do in my life is because I want to make my mum proud. There's no limit to what I would do for her.

SHE TAUGHT ME AND MY
SIBLINGS TO BE KIND, BUT NOT
TO BE NAIVE (THERE'S AN IMPORTANT
DIFFERENCE!). SHE WOULD TELL US TO BE
CAREFUL WHEN WE WENT OUTSIDE AND TO
ALWAYS LOOK AFTER ONE ANOTHER WHEN WE DID.
SHE WAS STRICT A LOT OF THE TIME, BUT THAT
WAS BECAUSE SHE HAD TO BE. I'M FOREVER PROUD
OF GROWING UP IN WITHINGTON AND WYTHENSHAWE
IN MANCHESTER, BUT THEY ARE TOUGH AREAS
TO LIVE IN IF YOU'RE NOT CAREFUL.
MY MUM KEPT US ALL GROUNDED AND
MADE SURE WE NEVER GOT TOO
BIG FOR OUR BOOTS.

She would tell us to be grateful for the good days and she always tried to keep us cheerful on the bad ones. It must have been so hard for her to do this on days when she was exhausted from working so much, but she never let us know. The world might have been a hard place outside, but my mum wanted to make sure that there was a lot of love inside our home.

That's the sort of person my mum is. She's kind, loving and always has time for other people.

SHE'S THE SORT OF PERSON THAT I TRY TO BE EVERY DAY OF MY LIFE.

I talk a lot about the importance of the journey we all take in life. But this is actually something that I learned from my mum. She's the one who first told me that everything we do is part of a journey. That every single experience in our life, the good and the bad, are all a part of us. That everything that happens to us on this journey helps to make us the people that we are, and combine to make us unique. Because while it's important to work hard and do what you can to move forward in your journey, you must also remember not to compare your journey to anyone else's.

There were times when my mum's journey didn't look so good. There have been times on my own journey when I've struggled. There were days that were tough for both of us.

I remember one summer – when things had been going OK for a while and we had a bit of money saved up – we were going to go on a family holiday. We were all so excited. We didn't often get to do things like go on holiday, so this was a real treat.

And then the washing machine broke. So my mum had to use all the money she'd saved up to buy a new one. Which meant we couldn't go on holiday.

I REMEMBER WONDERING IF WE WERE EVER GOING TO CATCH A BREAK.

Thankfully we are both at a point in our lives now where things are better, and we are always grateful for that. In fact, my mum and I like to think the bad days helped get us to where we are today. Without them, we would be different people and we might not have had the same opportunities, **SO IT'S IMPORTANT TO REMIND OURSELVES THAT THE BAD TIMES ARE JUST AS IMPORTANT AS THE GOOD ONES.**

(My mum has a caravan that she likes to take on holidays in Devon now. Whenever she makes the trip I give her some of her favourite chocolates — Ferrero Rocher — and she tells me she's the happiest person in the world!)

Let me put it to you this way: I grew up in Manchester. It rains a lot around here. And I mean A LOT. The skies are grey most of the time, and sometimes it gets so cold that you don't want to go outside. Growing up around here means you do things a certain way: all my jackets are waterproof, and I always pack an umbrella for long trips.

But when you grow up around so much rain, you get an appreciation for the days when the sun comes out. You make a special effort to see family or friends, have a little party or maybe even a barbecue. You make the most of the sunny days and celebrate when you can, so you have good memories to think about when the rain comes along again.

Even though the rainy days are tough, my mum made me understand they don't last forever. And even then, some of the prettiest flowers need rain from time to time to bloom.

BAD DAYS CAN COME AND GO, BUT BAD DAYS CAN ALSO HELP TO GIVE YOU THE EXPERIENCE AND LIFE KNOWLEDGE TO BECOME THE BEST VERSION OF YOURSELF.

I want you to be proud of your background. To be proud of where you came from. To make sure that you celebrate the good days and the good people you share them with.

TRY YOUR BEST TO REMEMBER THAT THE BAD DAYS WON'T LAST FOREVER WHEN THEY COME ALONG.

It's all part of the journey, and it all goes into making you the special and unique person you are.

THERE IS SO MUCH POTENTIAL WITHIN YOU RIGHT NOW

You get to decide who you want to be, and I hope that no matter what happens to you, you find time to be kind to people like my mum has done, and like I try to be as well. The way my mum explains it, when you wake up try and be the best version of yourself, no matter what you're trying to do. When we try to be our very best selves we can sleep a little bit better at night, knowing we gave it our all.

WE'RE NOT ALWAYS GOING TO BE AT 100 PER CENT EVERY DAY, BUT IT'S IMPORTANT TO KEEP TAKING STEPS FORWARD ON OUR JOURNEY.

Try not to get too worried about how fast or how slow things are happening, just know that when you try your best you shouldn't have any regrets. That way you'll know you've done all you can do.

With the other people I've talked about in this book, I've tried to show you one important way that they have impacted my life. But to be honest, I couldn't do that with my mum. There are just too many ways in which she's changed my life and helped me to become the person I am today. I wouldn't be where I am today if I didn't have her as my mum, on my team, supporting me every step of the way. Through the good days and the bad.

She's taught me to be kind and to help other people as much as I can. But beyond that, she's shown me how to appreciate every stage of my life's journey, as those are the experiences that make me, me. Everything I've been through in my life has added up to make me unique.

I want you to remember that as you go on your life's journey too. There might be a day when you are struggling at a particular lesson at school, or you have an argument with a friend, or you don't play as well as you normally do in football (or any other sport!). But remember that it's all part of the process. No journey is ever one smooth, straight line to the top. There will be bumps along the way, and things that set you back, but whenever these things happen you will learn from the experience, and come back stronger.

I try to talk to my mum every day. I tell her to put her feet up and just relax, but when you've been working so hard for so many years it becomes routine. Thankfully she doesn't have to work two jobs any more, but she's still doing bits and bobs and giving me advice on how I should sort out my post or clean my room. I just laugh whenever she does; I know she's only trying to help and I'm just glad she gets to be stress-free in her life now.

And that's all I could ask for. She's inspired me in so many ways, so it's nice to be able to look after her now. Remember, the rainy days will come, but afterwards you'll appreciate the sunny days so much more. It's all part of the journey.

MY FINAL HERO

10

THIS IS IT.
THE END OF THE BOOK.

You might have already flicked to this page early or wondered who the final hero was going to be.

Was it going to be a football player? Or a musician? Was it going to be a YouTuber? Or someone who I'm really close to, like my brothers or sisters?

Well, the truth is, the final hero of this book is someone I haven't met yet. But they're someone I hear a lot about.

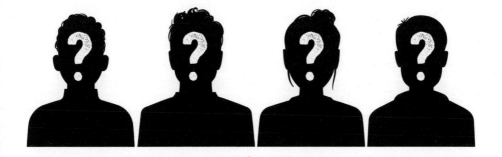

They're someone who is kind, brave and always trying their best. They're a person who cares a lot about others and who tries to help when possible.

They're funny, and they like to remind the people around them of the brighter side of life.

They're really inspiring too. They're someone who doesn't get too downbeat when there are bad days, and they're also someone who celebrates loudly when the good times come.

They don't settle. They know things could be better, but they don't get angry when things go wrong.

They don't mind taking on big challenges, even when they sound scary. And they're a person who can keep their team strong when things look a bit shaky.

They're a good friend in good times and bad.

I really want to meet them, but I know I'll have to get in the queue because *everyone* wants to meet them.

I hope that if we ever do meet, they'll know that I think they're really inspiring. I want them to know that I've been rooting for them for a long time. I think they're going to go on to do incredible things.

HAVE YOU FIGURED OUT WHO THE PERSON IS YET . . . ?

THE FINAL HERO
OF THIS BOOK IS

YOU

BECAUSE THE TRUTH IS, YOU ARE THE HERO OF THIS BOOK. YOU, THE PERSON HOLDING THIS BOOK RIGHT NOW. I WANT YOU TO KNOW THAT YOU HAVE THE POTENTIAL TO BE THE HERO OF YOUR OWN LIFE.

WITHIN YOU RIGHT NOW
IS THE POWER TO OWN
YOUR OWN STORY

I've talked a lot about how I think it's important to have role models and people to look up to in life, but remember that the people who inspire you don't have to be a celebrity or someone with lots of money.

There are inspiring people all around you. All you have to do is look and listen as best you can. And if you can do that, if you can find heroes in lots of different places, you'll discover that you are a hero too. And that you can in turn inspire the people around you.

I'm really fortunate that I grew up with a ton of inspiring people around me. My mum taught me the importance of kindness and hard work. My grandmother encouraged me to always ask questions. My older brothers got me into football, and my older sisters taught me so many things about the big wide world beyond football.

Today, I still have my family around me, inspiring me, but I'm lucky enough to have a whole new family too: my friends who empower me to be the best version of myself that I can be, and my teammates who are always there to push me.

I wouldn't be the person I am today without all of these amazing people, along with everyone else included in this book. All of them have played a role in my life, inspiring me and helping to guide me on my own personal journey. I don't think I could have achieved all of the things I have done — be it in football, campaigning or even writing books — without all of these incredible heroes.

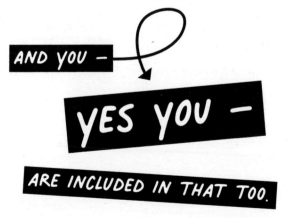

AND YOU —

YES YOU —

ARE INCLUDED IN THAT TOO.

As I said right at the very start of this book, one of my favourite things is meeting a new person and hearing them talk about their life's journey. It's taught me that every person in this world is so different and that all of our stories and experiences are unique.

I MIGHT NOT HAVE MET YOU YET, BUT I KNOW YOUR STORY IS SPECIAL. I KNOW THAT YOU HAVE ONLY JUST BEGUN TO TELL IT.

That thought inspires me. It makes me want to do better and to help you tell your story. That's why I've tried my hardest to campaign and champion others, and why I always try to listen and learn where possible.

So, I'm ending this book by telling you that I am listening. I hope that one day you will get to tell your own amazing story to someone you meet. You could tell them about the hero you decided to be and all of the ways you looked to help people.

The world around you is listening. You might not have noticed it yet, but it's happening. There are people in your life right now who are trying their best to help guide you on your personal journey. If you tell them the story you want to tell and listen to the advice they give you, you'll be amazed by what happens next. You can find inspiration anywhere you look. In each other and in yourself. You don't need lots of money or fame to make a difference.

I'm not going to pretend that it will be easy for you, or that success will happen overnight. You will encounter setbacks, and there will be problems along the way.

But I think the key to being a good hero is not being afraid of making mistakes or getting too worried about problems you may face in life. It is being open to finding lots of different ways to solve those problems.

That is important. That, to me, is the bravery you hear about in so many heroes, be they from history books, comic books, movies, famous people you see on TV, or even people you know at school or in your local area.

EVERY HERO IS DRIVEN BY A DESIRE TO WANT TO HELP OTHERS AND SOLVE PROBLEMS.

They're someone who is able to take a deep breath when things are going wrong, instead of giving up.

They're someone who can look within to try and think of ways to help, and look to others and let them know they want to work together. As a team. As a community. As a collective.

A HERO IS SOMEONE WHO CAN TAKE A STEP FORWARD WHEN THINGS ARE BAD, WHILE TURNING BACK AND HOLDING OUT A HELPING HAND TO ANYONE BEHIND THEM.

I hope to one day be that type of person. That is what drives and inspires me a lot of the time. And I think you can be that person. I hope that knowledge drives and inspires you too.

You can be the hero of your own life. So as you go out into the big wide world, I want you to remember a few important things:

TRY TO SURROUND YOURSELF WITH HEROES WHO INSPIRE YOU

MAKE AN EFFORT TO SURROUND YOURSELF WITH HEROES WHO MOTIVATE YOU

BE A HERO FOR OTHERS, AND MOTIVATE AND INSPIRE THEM IN RETURN

IF YOU CAN DO ALL OF THAT, YOU'RE ALREADY BEING THE BEST VERSION OF YOURSELF THAT YOU CAN BE.

SO GO OUT THERE AND BE THE CHANGE.

MR

ABOUT THE AUTHORS

Marcus Rashford MBE

Marcus Rashford MBE is Manchester United's iconic number 10 and an England International footballer.

During the lockdown imposed due to the COVID-19 pandemic, Marcus teamed up with the food distribution charity FareShare to cover the free school meal deficit for vulnerable children across the UK, raising in excess of 20 million pounds. Marcus successfully lobbied the British Government to U-turn policy around the free food voucher programme – a campaign that has been deemed the quickest turnaround of government policy in the history of British politics – so that 1.3 million vulnerable children continued to have access to food supplies whilst schools were closed during the pandemic.

In response to Marcus's End Child Food Poverty campaign, the British Government committed £400 million to support vulnerable children across the UK, supporting 1.7 million children for the next 12 months. In October 2020, he was appointed MBE in the Queen's Birthday Honours. Marcus has committed himself to combating child poverty in the UK and his books *You Are a Champion*, *You Can Do It*, and *The Marcus Rashford You Are a Champion Action Planner* are inspiring guides for children about reaching their full potential.

Marcus is also the author of the bestselling The Breakfast Club Adventures, a fiction series that inspires a love of reading in kids and shows them that adventure can be found anywhere.

Carl Anka

Carl Anka is a London-born journalist and broadcaster who likes his tea with milk and one sugar. He has written for the **BBC,** *The Guardian*, *VICE*, *NME*, *GQ* and *BuzzFeed* among other publications online and in print, and specialises in writing about pop culture, video games, films and football. Currently a reporter for sports media group *The Athletic*, covering Manchester United, he is the host of the *Talk of the Devils* podcast and is scared of talking on the phone.

Along with Marcus Rashford, Carl is the co-writer of *You Are a Champion* and its follow-up *You Can Do It* — positive and inspiring guides for life for young readers.

Have you read Marcus Rashford's bestselling non-fiction series?

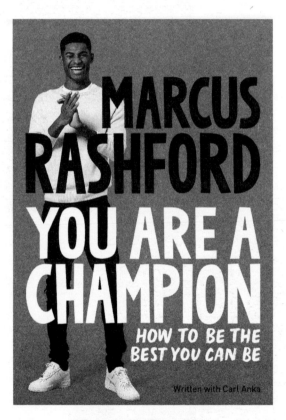

The Number One Bestseller

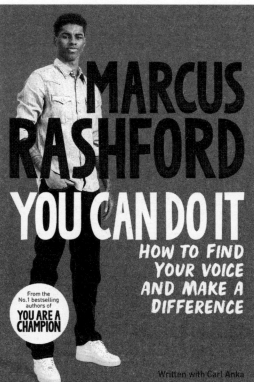

MARCUS RASHFORD

YOU CAN DO IT

HOW TO FIND YOUR VOICE AND MAKE A DIFFERENCE

From the No.1 bestselling authors of **YOU ARE A CHAMPION**

Written with Carl Anka

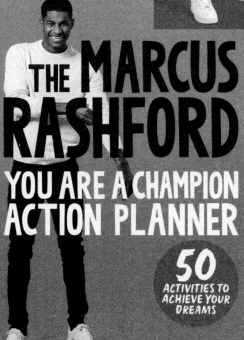

THE MARCUS RASHFORD

YOU ARE A CHAMPION ACTION PLANNER

50 ACTIVITIES TO ACHIEVE YOUR DREAMS

Written with Katie Warriner

THERE'S SOMETHING STRANGE GOING ON AT SCHOOL . . .

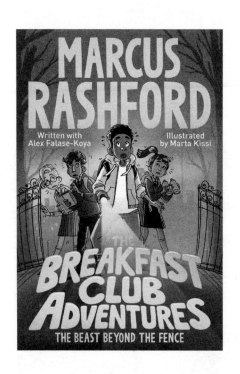

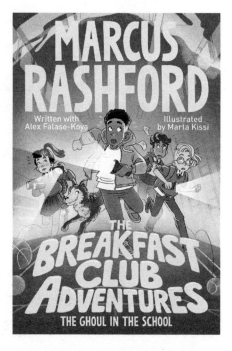

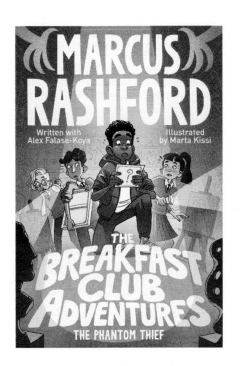

OUT MARCH 2024

DON'T MISS MARCUS RASHFORD'S BESTSELLING FICTION SERIES, THE BREAKFAST CLUB ADVENTURES!